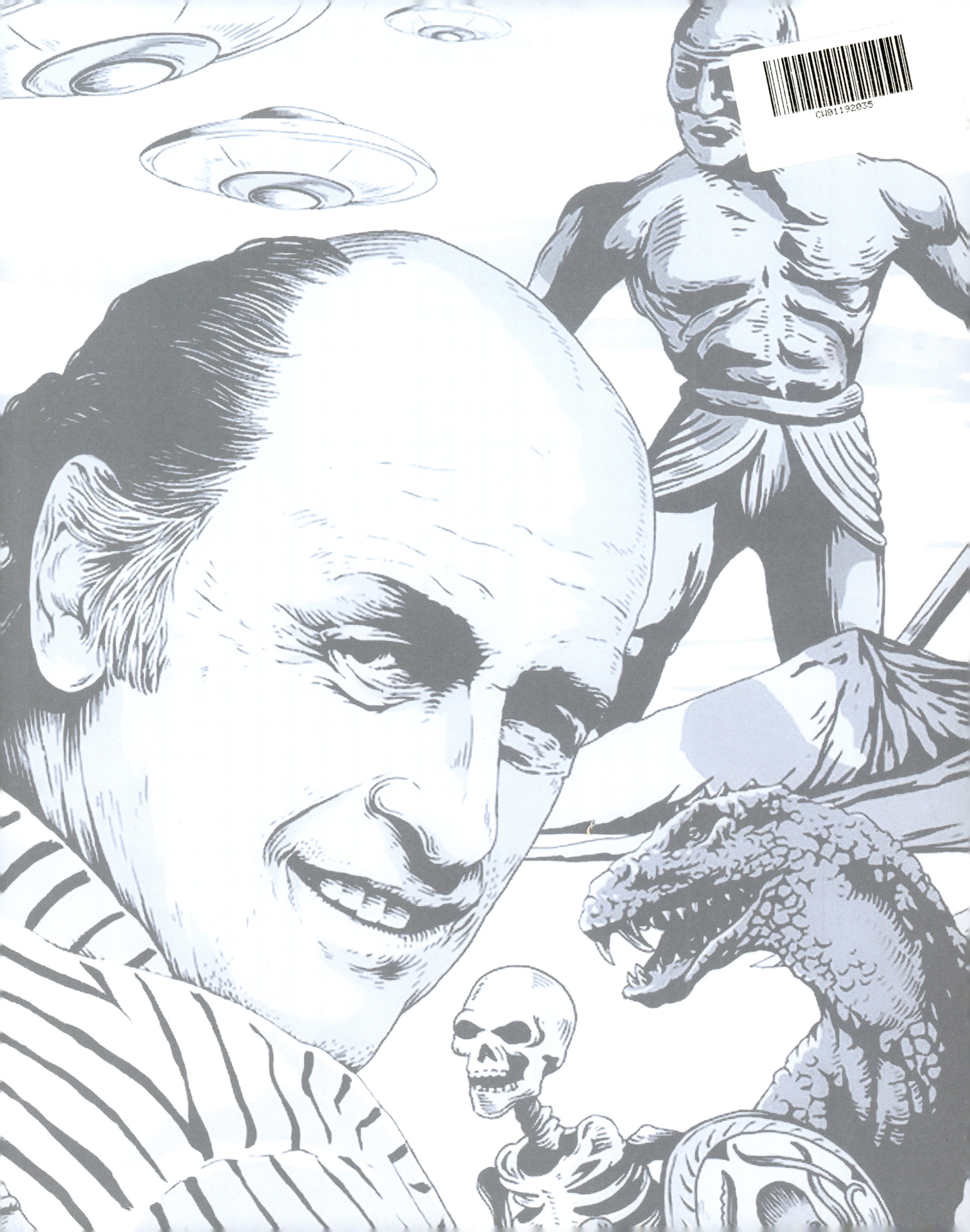

HARRYHAUSEN
THE MOVIE POSTERS

**For my lovely wife Christine Ann,
without whom none of this would have been possible.**

HARRYHAUSEN
THE MOVIE POSTERS

ISBN: 9781785656781

Published by Titan Books
A division of Titan Publishing Group Ltd.
144 Southwark St.
London
SE1 0UP

First edition: September 2018
10 9 8 7 6 5 4 3 2 1

Photos on Foreword ©John Landis
Photo on Page 9 ©AMPAS

To receive advance information, news, competitions, and exclusive offers online,
please sign up for the Titan newsletter on our website: www.titanbooks.com

Did you enjoy this book? We love to hear from our readers.
Please e-mail us at: readerfeedback@titanemail.com or write to
Reader Feedback at the above address.

No part of this publication may be reproduced, stored in a retrieval system, or transmitted, in any form or by any means without the prior written permission of the publisher, nor be otherwise circulated in any form of binding or cover other than that in which it is published and without a similar condition being imposed on the subsequent purchaser.

A CIP catalogue record for this title is available from the British Library.

Printed and bound in China.

FOR THOSE READERS INTERESTED IN FINDING OUT MORE ABOUT RAY'S LIFE AND WORK:

Ray Harryhausen: Master of the Majicks by Mike Hankin, Archive Editions.
Ray Harryhausen: An Animated Life by Ray Harryhausen and Tony Dalton, Aurum.
The Art of Ray Harryhausen by Ray Harryhausen and Tony Dalton, Aurum.
Ray Harryhausen: The Master of Movie Magic by Richard Holliss, Ghoulish Pub.
Action Man by Richard Holliss, WVIP Pub.

More about Ray and his legacy is available online at **www.rayharryhausen.com**
The Ray & Diana Harryhausen Foundation (charity number SC001419)

Posters in this book are courtesy of the following companies:
King Kong © RKO Pictures Inc. *Mighty Joe Young* 1949 (An Arko Production) © RKO Pictures Inc. All Rights Reserved. *The Beast From 20,000 Fathoms* 1953, renewed 1981 © Warner Brothers Entertainment Inc. All Rights Reserved *The Animal World* 1955, renewed 1983, © Warner Brothers Entertainment Inc. All Rights Reserved. *The Valley of Gwangi* 1969, renewed 1997 © Warner Brothers Entertainment Inc. All Rights Reserved. *Clash of the Titans* 1981 © Turner Entertainment Co. A Warner Brothers Entertainment Company. All Rights Reserved. *It Came From Beneath the Sea* 1955, renewed 1983. *Earth Vs. the Flying Saucers* 1956 (A Clover Production), renewed 1984. *20 Million Miles To Earth* 1957, renewed 1986. *The 7th Voyage of Sinbad* 1958 (A Morningside Production), renewed 1986. *The 3 Worlds of Gulliver* 1960 (A Morningside Production), renewed 1988. *Mysterious Island* 1961 (An Ameran Film), renewed 1989. *Jason and the Argonauts* 1963 (A Morningside Worldwide Pictures S.A.), renewed 1991. *First Men in the Moon* 1964 (An Ameran Film), renewed 1992. *The Golden Voyage of Sinbad* 1973, renewed 2001. *Sinbad and the Eye of the Tiger* 1977 © Columbia Pictures Industries Inc. All Rights Reserved. *One Million Years B.C.* 1966, Hammer Films Productions Ltd. Canal+Image Ltd. All Rights Reserved.

HARRYHAUSEN
THE MOVIE POSTERS

RICHARD HOLLISS
Foreword by JOHN LANDIS

The Ray and Diana Harryhausen Foundation

TITAN BOOKS

CONTENTS

FOREWORD: 06

INTRODUCTION: 08

CHAPTER ONE: 12
MIGHTY JOE YOUNG

CHAPTER TWO: 26
THE BEAST FROM 20,000 FATHOMS

CHAPTER THREE: 34
IT CAME FROM BENEATH THE SEA

CHAPTER FOUR: 44
THE ANIMAL WORLD

CHAPTER FIVE: 50
EARTH VS. THE FLYING SAUCERS
20 MILLION MILES TO EARTH

CHAPTER SIX: 68
THE 7TH VOYAGE OF SINBAD

CHAPTER SEVEN: 82
THE 3 WORLDS OF GULLIVER
MYSTERIOUS ISLAND

CHAPTER EIGHT: 102
JASON AND THE ARGONAUTS

CHAPTER NINE: 114
FIRST MEN IN THE MOON

CHAPTER TEN: 126
ONE MILLION YEARS B.C.
THE VALLEY OF GWANGI

CHAPTER ELEVEN: 150
THE GOLDEN VOYAGE OF SINBAD
SINBAD AND THE EYE OF THE TIGER

CHAPTER TWELVE: 166
CLASH OF THE TITANS

CHAPTER THIRTEEN: 182
RAY HARRYHAUSEN: SPECIAL EFFECTS TITAN

THE RAY & DIANA HARRYHAUSEN FOUNDATION: 190

SELECT INDEX: 192

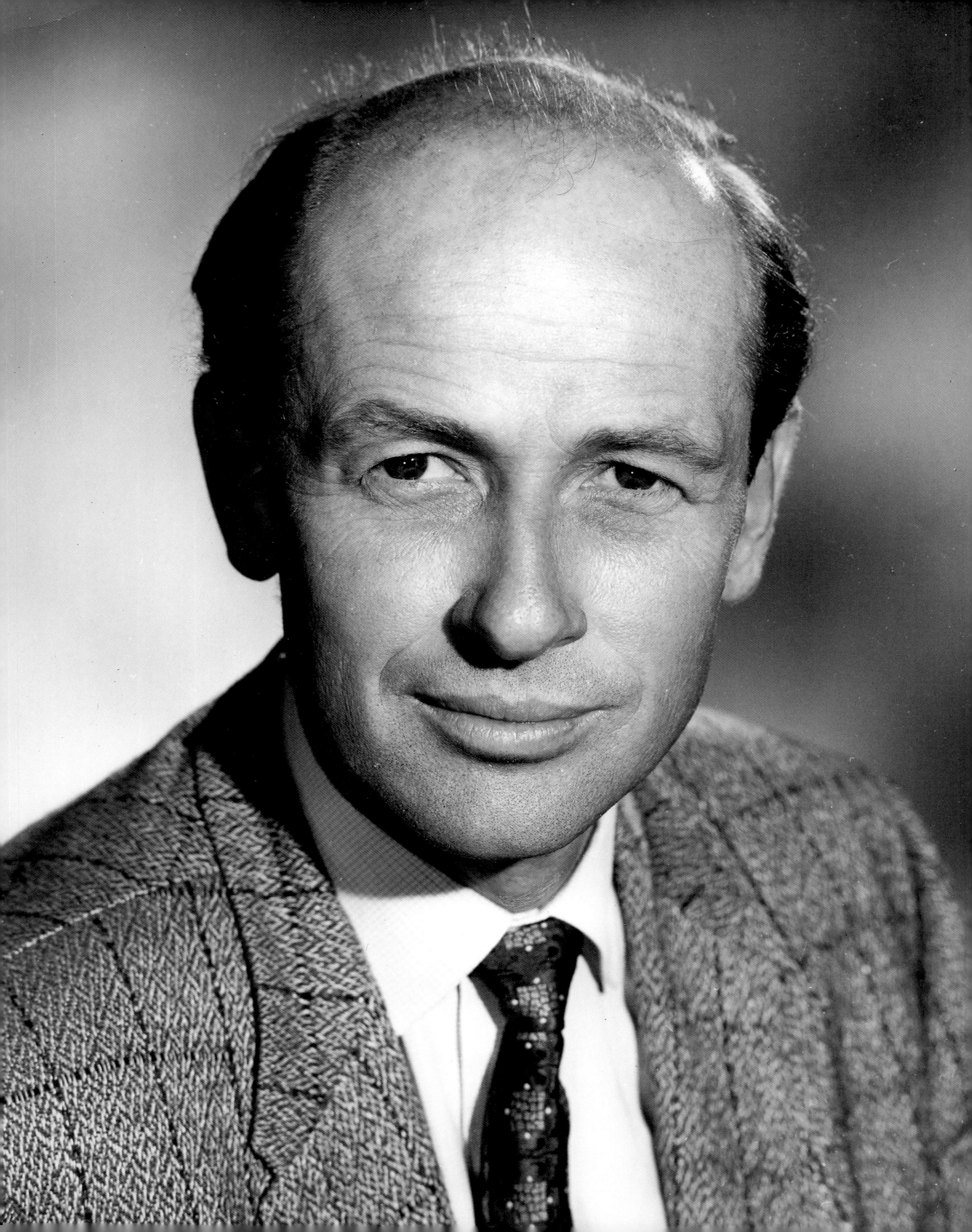

FOREWORD
BY JOHN LANDIS

Ray Harryhausen's singular legacy is celebrated by the posters and advertising art reproduced in this volume. As Ray was inspired by seeing the original *King Kong*, so too were generations of filmmakers inspired by his body of work. Countless directors, writers, make-up artists, and especially visual effects artists regard Ray as their mentor and muse.

Many of Ray's creatures are so unique that their image can instantly identify the film in which they appeared: the powerful Cyclops from *The Seventh Voyage of Sinbad*; the towering bronze warrior Talos from *Jason and the Argonauts*; the mythical dinosaur Rhedosaurus; the title creature from *The Beast From 20,000 Fathoms*; the charming gorilla named *Mighty Joe Young*, and so many more are illustrated in the lavish advertising art collected here. The photographs and artists' impressions remind us of the artistry and excitement of those wonderful movies.

Terry Gilliam once said that Ray Harryhausen was the first 'digital artist' because all his creations were literally created with his 'digits'. Terry points out that Ray's work was completely handcrafted; Ray sculpted, painted and manipulated each figure into life one frame at a time.

Whether you read this book as a fan or film scholar, think of these marvellous posters and advertisement art as an invitation to view Ray's work once more.

THIS SPREAD: (Opposite) Ray Harryhausen. (Above) John Landis and Ray Harryhausen. (Below) British Quad double-bill poster for *Jason and the Argonauts/Siege of the Saxons* (1963). Courtesy of Simon Greetham Archive.

INTRODUCTION

In 1992, the Academy of Motion Picture Arts and Sciences finally recognized the outstanding contribution that animator Ray Harryhausen had made to the art of special effects cinematography by making him the ninth recipient of the coveted Gordon E. Sawyer award (named after the former sound director at MGM and three-time Academy Award™ winner). In a special presentation, actor Tom Hanks, a self-confessed Harryhausen fan, summed up the sentiments of countless movie fans and industry insiders when he opined, "Some people say *Casablanca* or *Citizen Kane*. I say *Jason and the Argonauts* was the greatest film ever made!" Hanks' comments couldn't have been more timely. For while Ray's films had been totally ignored for years by the Academy, his proprietary brand of stop-motion special effects, called Dynamation (in which miniature three-dimensional figures are moved one frame at a time to create the illusion of movement), was receiving unreserved praise from the likes of Steven Spielberg, George Lucas, James Cameron, John Landis and Peter Jackson.

Ten years later in 2003 (the 70th anniversary of the pioneering stop-motion special effects classic *King Kong*) Ray was invited back to Hollywood to attend the unveiling ceremony of his star on the famous Hollywood Walk of Fame.

It wasn't just a coincidence that the individuals who contacted the Chamber of Commerce to nominate Ray for such an accolade chose 2003 to commemorate Ray's achievements with a permanent name check adjacent to the famous Graumann's Chinese Theater on Hollywood Boulevard. For it was in this very theater seven decades earlier that the young Harryhausen was to shape his destiny.

THIS PAGE: (Above) Ray and a model ceratosaurus from *The Animal World* (1956). (Below) The author Richard Holliss poses with the life-size statue of the animator that was unveiled at his 90th birthday party.

HARRYHAUSEN THE MOVIE POSTERS

Slim and rather tall for his age, thirteen-year-old dinosaur enthusiast Ray sat spellbound as the magic of motion pictures transported him to the steaming jungles of a lost island off the coast of Sumatra. Here in a land of hostile natives resided not only a menagerie of monstrous prehistoric creatures, but the 'Eighth Wonder of the World' — a giant gorilla called King Kong. Perched on the edge of his seat, his eyes glued to the screen, the awe-struck youngster suddenly realized that his life was about to change forever.

But there was more to this movie than just the spectacle and breathtaking visual effects. *King Kong* was released in the second decade of the golden age of film promotion, at a time when films were marketed with imagination and flare. The Chinese Theater's lavish foyer display for *King Kong* was almost as exciting as the film itself. The publicity department at RKO, the studio responsible for financing the movie, had transformed the lobby into a jungle set with creepers and vines surrounding elaborate displays of full-color posters and photographs from the film.

> **Ray's movies were a publicist's dream, with amazing and diverse artwork created to promote his films.**

And just as Ray had been lured into the theater by all the razzamatazz generated by the studio's marketing department, so audiences over the years have also been drawn to their local cinemas by grand poster designs and illuminated marquee displays. This vital ingredient in the selling of films is often referred to in campaign books (special publications filled with promotional ideas that are issued exclusively to cinemas) as 'ballyhoo'. *King Kong* was a prime example. Fortunately, this type of marketing lasted almost as long as Ray was making films, so his movies usually had some spectacular artwork to publicize their release. In fact, *Mighty Joe Young* (1949), the first feature-length film on which he worked, received just as much 'ballyhoo' as *King Kong* had seventeen years earlier.

And it was this same 'ballyhoo' that continued to sell Ray's unique style of filmmaking for all the movies that followed between 1953 and 1981. Film posters were the key selling point and as this book shows, Ray's movies were a publicist's dream, with amazing and diverse artwork created to promote his films from *The Beast From 20,000 Fathoms* to *Clash of the Titans*.

By the 1950s, film poster art had moved on from showing Bogart and Bacall, Turner and Gable, Karloff and Lugosi. Billboards and cinema marquees were filled with full-color paintings depicting dinosaurs demolishing modern cities, a multi-tentacled sea beast toppling the Golden Gate Bridge, a giant spaceship plunging into the ocean, monsters locked in mortal combat, or a muscle-bound hero sword fighting with a skeleton warrior. All these strange and exciting images were adorning the foyers of cinemas worldwide, while posters of all shapes and sizes were looming down at cinemagoers on street corners and from the sides of buildings.

THIS PAGE: (Left) Ray receiving his Oscar® (the Gordon E. Sawyer Award) from actor Tom Hanks in 1992.

INTRODUCTION

10

This book, therefore, is a celebration of that artwork, the stuff of dreams. And while the names of some of the illustrators responsible have been lost in the mists of time, there are also some fine examples of poster art by renowned artists from across Europe and America. These included established illustrators and painters, such as Greg and Tim Hildebrandt, whose atmospheric painting for Ray's 1981 mythological adventure *Clash of the Titans* is much sought after by collectors, or Italian Anselmo Ballester, whose interpretations of Ray's 1950s science fiction movies evoke a remarkable sense of wonder. And who could forget that iconic image from the mid-1960s of actress Raquel Welch, wearing the flimsiest of fur bikinis, by UK artist Tom Chantrell for Hammer's *One Million Years B.C.*? Amazing examples of the surreal style of mid-European artists such as Jacek Neugebaur and Olga Fischerová are also included, from *The Golden Voyage of Sinbad*.

These stunning and evocative posters also tell us a great deal about how the movie industry has changed. Thanks to social media, television and streaming, 21st century filmmakers don't have to rely on in-house publicity departments any more. Modern cinemas are no longer the grand palaces of old, with thousands of seats, lush carpeting and foyers filled with tantalising examples of good old-fashioned ballyhoo, but are instead cramped multiplexes with CinemaScope-wide confectionary counters.

Showmanship, which was once such an integral part of film marketing, has been lost. Which is probably why the film posters of yesteryear are in great demand from collectors worldwide. Hundreds, even thousands of dollars exchange hands at auctions and poster conventions for film posters that are every bit as vital and amazing as the films they promote.

Looking through the posters that I've selected for this book, I hope that you'll agree. For not only are they all superb examples of the magic of cinema, but a celebration of the genius of Ray Harryhausen.

Richard Holliss, 2018

THIS SPREAD: PAGE 10: (Clockwise from Top Left) *It Came From Beneath the Sea*, *Earth Vs. The Flying Saucers*, *The Golden Voyage of Sinbad*, *The Valley of Gwangi*
THIS PAGE: (Top) Ray with two of the stunning pre-production drawings he created for the film *The 7th Voyage of Sinbad* (1958). (Left) Ray relaxing in his studio in his West London home.

INTRODUCTION

CHAPTER ONE

MIGHTY JOE YOUNG (1949)

FIRST TECHNICIAN: RAY HARRYHAUSEN

New York nightclub owner Max O'Hara visits Africa to capture wild animals to entertain his guests. Impressed by Jill Young's pet gorilla, Joe, he persuades her to swap their idyllic life in the Congo for a well-paid job in America. But when Joe is served alcohol by some drunken revelers he goes berserk, destroying the nightclub and endangering many lives. When the authorities insist that Joe must be destroyed, Jill and cowboy Gregg Ford hatch a plan to sneak the gorilla aboard a cargo ship bound for Africa. Joe is finally allowed to leave after he bravely rescues a group of children from a blazing orphanage.

MIGHTIER THAN KING KONG!

Born in Los Angeles on June 29th 1920, Ray Harryhausen grew up with a passion for film, literature, art and music. But it was *King Kong* (1933) and its innovative model animation — in which miniature articulated models of prehistoric animals were photographed one frame at a time to simulate movement — that really fired his imagination. Building his own models and shooting a series of experimental films led to a chance meeting with special effects technician Willis O'Brien, the pioneering genius responsible for the groundbreaking effects in both *King Kong* and the 1925 silent version of Sir Arthur Conan Doyle's *The Lost World*.

Encouraged by O'Brien to turn his enthusiasm for stop-motion animation into a chosen profession, Ray continued working on a number of solo projects and experimental films, before joining Hungarian producer George Pal. Pal — who would later mastermind some of the most influential science fiction films of the 1950s, including *Destination Moon*, *When Worlds Collide,* and *The War of the Worlds* — assigned the young animator to work on his famous *Puppetoon* series (1932–1948).

A short while later, Ray was employed by director Frank Capra (*It's A Wonderful Life*) as an assistant cameraman and special effects technician on the classic wartime propaganda series *Why We Fight*. In the mid 1940s, Ray also began work on the first in a series of stop-motion shorts, which were based on famous nursery rhymes, called *The Mother Goose Stories*.

THIS PAGE: (Above) The manager of the Plaza cinema in Maidenhead, England, demonstrates the versatility of a 48-sheet size poster with this impressive window display. (Below) A 1952 US Half-sheet re-release poster for *King Kong*.

HARRYHAUSEN THE MOVIE POSTERS

While working alone, Ray kept in contact with O'Brien and was thrilled to discover that RKO, the company responsible for producing the original *King Kong*, were planning a new stop-motion film about another giant gorilla called *Mighty Joe Young*.

The idea was the brainchild of veteran Hollywood producer Merian C. Cooper, an explorer-cum-filmmaker who had been responsible for the original *King Kong*. He assigned O'Brien to outline what was required to create the film's complex special effects and, after a great deal of preliminary work, the project was green-lit by the studio on a budget of 1.5 million dollars.

O'Brien supervised both the stop-motion scenes and the film's other special effects in conjunction with the director Ernest B. Schoedsack (*King Kong, Dr. Cyclops*). Actor Robert Armstrong (who had played film producer Carl Denham in both *King Kong* and the sequel *Son of Kong*) was cast in the lead as entrepreneur Max O'Hara, with Terry Moore (*The Great Rupert*) as Joe's carer, Jill Young, and Ben Johnson (*She Wore a Yellow Ribbon*) as O'Hara's business partner, Gregg Ford.

A special effects studio was set up on the RKO Pathé lot in Culver City and O'Brien's former model-making team, headed by Marcel Delgado (*King Kong*) constructed the

> **It was Ray's animation that, through subtle nuances and human-like gestures, allowed audiences to empathize with Joe.**

stop-motion models. Six different-sized versions of Joe were made, with a body manufactured from foam rubber and cotton, and built over flexible aluminum armatures. This was then covered with a rubberized furry hide.

The stop-motion work and other post-production special effects took almost fourteen months to complete, with Ray animating Joe's first jungle appearance, in which he attacks a lion cage. O'Brien and Ray combined real footage of the king of the beasts with a detailed model, and the result is seamless. Ray also worked on the complex scene in which Joe is lassoed. This could only be achieved by a combination of spilt-second timing and careful choreography of the live-action footage to match the movements of the men on horseback with the stop-motion figure. It's a brilliantly accomplished scene and one that Ray would resurrect twenty years later, substituting a dinosaur for a gorilla in *The Valley of Gwangi* (1969).

Even though other talented stop-motion technicians such as Pete Peterson (*Behemoth, The Sea Monster*) also worked on the film, it was Ray's animation that, through subtle nuances and human-like gestures, allowed audiences to empathize with Joe's character. Ray's skill as an animator, which was already on a par with O'Brien's work on *King Kong*, was similar to that of a film cartoonist who instills his own personality into a series of lifeless pencil drawings.

THIS PAGE: A 1956 US One-sheet re-release poster for *King Kong*.

CHAPTER ONE **MIGHTY JOE YOUNG**

NO MONSTER EVER LIVED THAT COULD
SEE...IN ACTION the power that could pulverize a city!
John Ford and Merian C. Cooper present
MIGHTY JOE YOUNG
MERIAN COOPER'S AMAZING ADVENTURE IN THE UNUSUAL!
starring
TERRY MOORE · BEN JOHNSON
and ROBERT ARMSTRONG with FRANK McHUGH
Directed by ERNEST B. SCHOEDSACK
Technical Creator Willis O'Brien • Screen Play by RUTH ROSE
An Arko Production • Re-released by RKO Radio Pictures, Inc.
Copyright 1953 RKO Radio Pictures Inc. Country of Origin U. S. A.

For the climax of the picture Ray animated some of the key scenes in which Joe rescues a child from a burning orphanage. O'Brien's team constructed an eight-foot-high plaster miniature of the building, which was filmed at high speed to create a more realistic fire effect. And although the film was made in black and white, these scenes were rendered more exciting by adding a red tint to the theatrical prints.

Mighty Joe Young opened in America in July 1949, after almost two years in production, and won the Academy Award™ for Best Special Effects. While not as popular as *King Kong*, the film was well received by the critics, and certainly captured the public's imagination thanks to a tremendous amount of advertising.

In America alone, the RKO publicity department produced four completely different 24-sheet (274x609cm) billboard-size posters, a single 12-sheet poster (138x304cm), two versions of the six-sheet (206x206cm), three different three-sheets (104x206cm), a single one-sheet (69x104cm), two half-sheets (56x71cm), and one insert card.

With bylines such as 'Staggering Sensation!', 'Electrifying Excitement!', 'It's Alive!', 'Mightier Than *King Kong*!', and the more ambiguous 'A powder-keg pet of night-club society', some of the publicity took a softer, more comedic approach. In one poster, Joe is seen demonstrating his amazing strength by holding a piano above his head, while alternative designs exploited the giant gorilla's battle with a pride of lions, or the explosive climax to the film in which he rescues a child from a blazing inferno.

Although it was advertised as a children's film in America (it double-billed in some territories with an adult drama called *A Woman's Secret*) the UK censor saw fit to cut the film, even with an A certificate. It then toured on the Gaumont cinema circuit, on a double-bill with a sports drama called *Duke of Chicago*, in January 1950.

Mighty Joe Young was successfully re-released in America in 1953 and later throughout Europe. This time the poster artists concentrated on the Wild West theme, including the cowboy lassoing sequence. The Italian poster (*Il Re Dell'Africa*), on the other hand, showed Joe bursting out of the jungle whilst simultaneously clutching a damsel-in-distress and battling lions. But at least the European artwork was more spectacular than distributor New Realm's 1959 UK re-release, which opted instead for a poster featuring a comically drawn gorilla on a sickly green-colored background. *Mighty Joe Young* also has the distinction of being the first of Ray's films ever to be shown on British television, with a commercial channel screening in 1964.

THIS SPREAD: The US Half-sheet for the 1953 re-release of *Mighty Joe Young* focused on the action sequences. Courtesy of Mike Hankin Archive.

CHAPTER ONE **MIGHTY JOE YOUNG**

HARRYHAUSEN THE MOVIE POSTERS

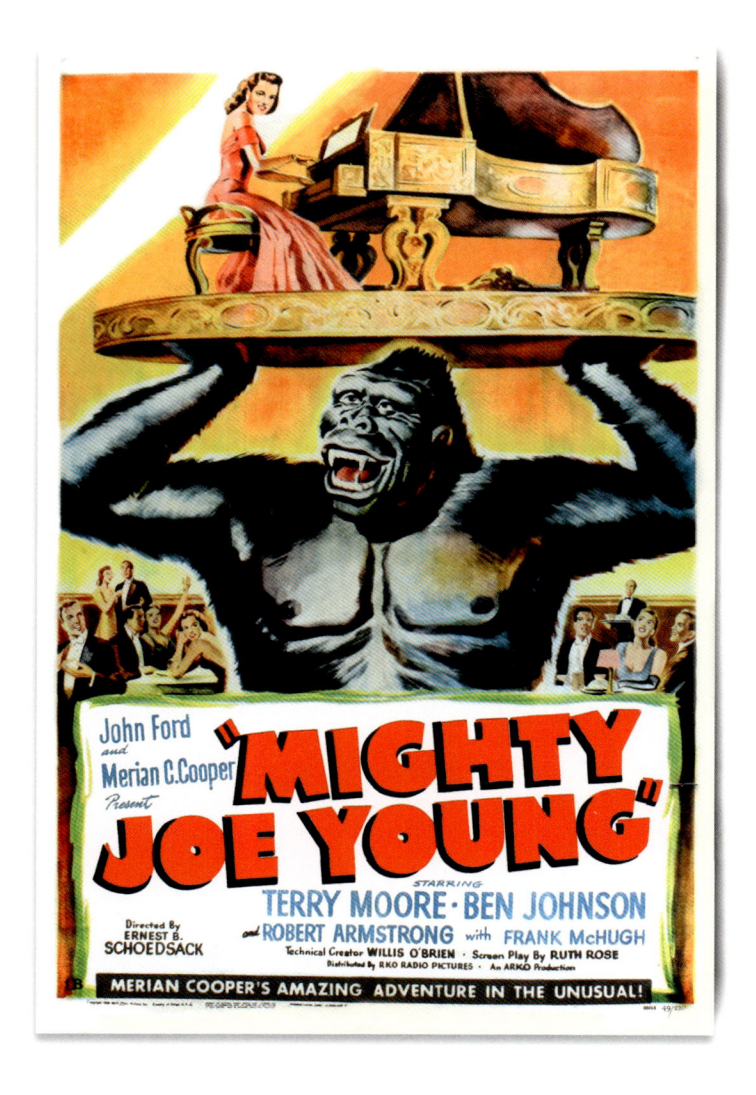

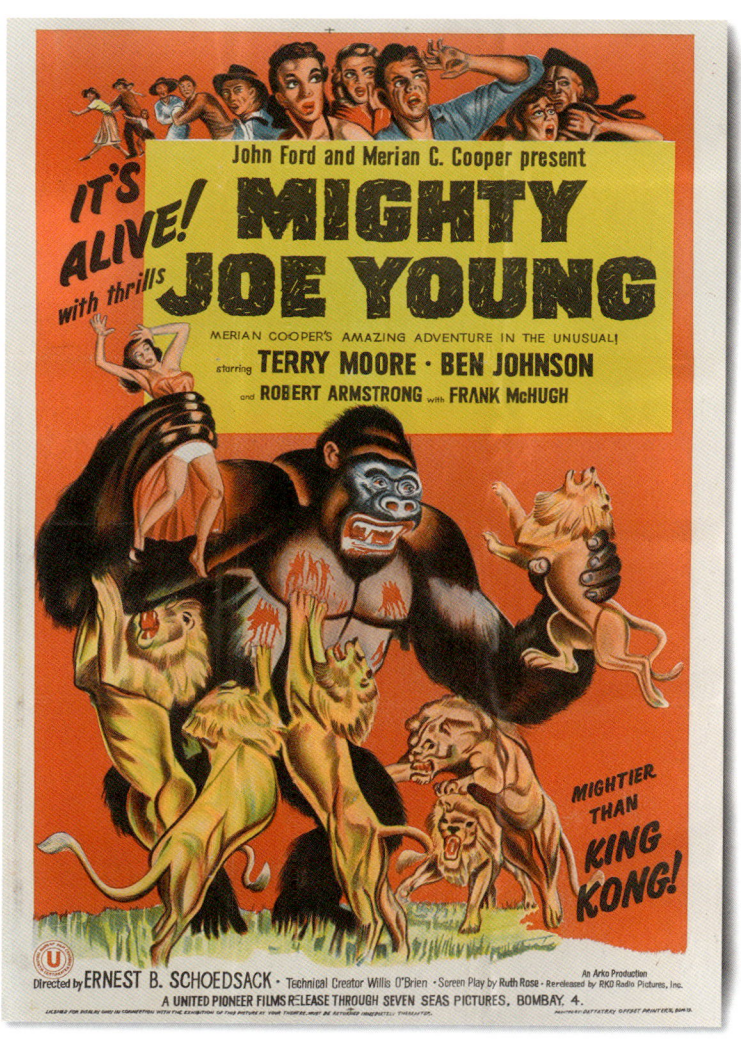

CHAPTER ONE **MIGHTY JOE YOUNG**

PREVIOUS SPREAD: PAGE 18 (Clockwise from Top Left) US One-sheet Style B (69 x 104cm). US One-sheet Style C (69 x 104cm) Art by Gene Widhoff. Indian One-sheet (69 x 104cm) Courtesy of Simon Greetham Archive. Spanish (64 x 98cm) Art by Jano. PAGE 19 British Double-crown (51 x 76cm).

THIS SPREAD: (Above) Italian Locandina (35 x 68cm) Courtesy of Neil Pettigrew Archive. (Right) US Half-sheet Style A (56 x 71cm) Art by Gene Widhoff.

HARRYHAUSEN THE MOVIE POSTERS

CHAPTER ONE **MIGHTY JOE YOUNG**

HARRYHAUSEN THE MOVIE POSTERS

CHAPTER ONE **MIGHTY JOE YOUNG**

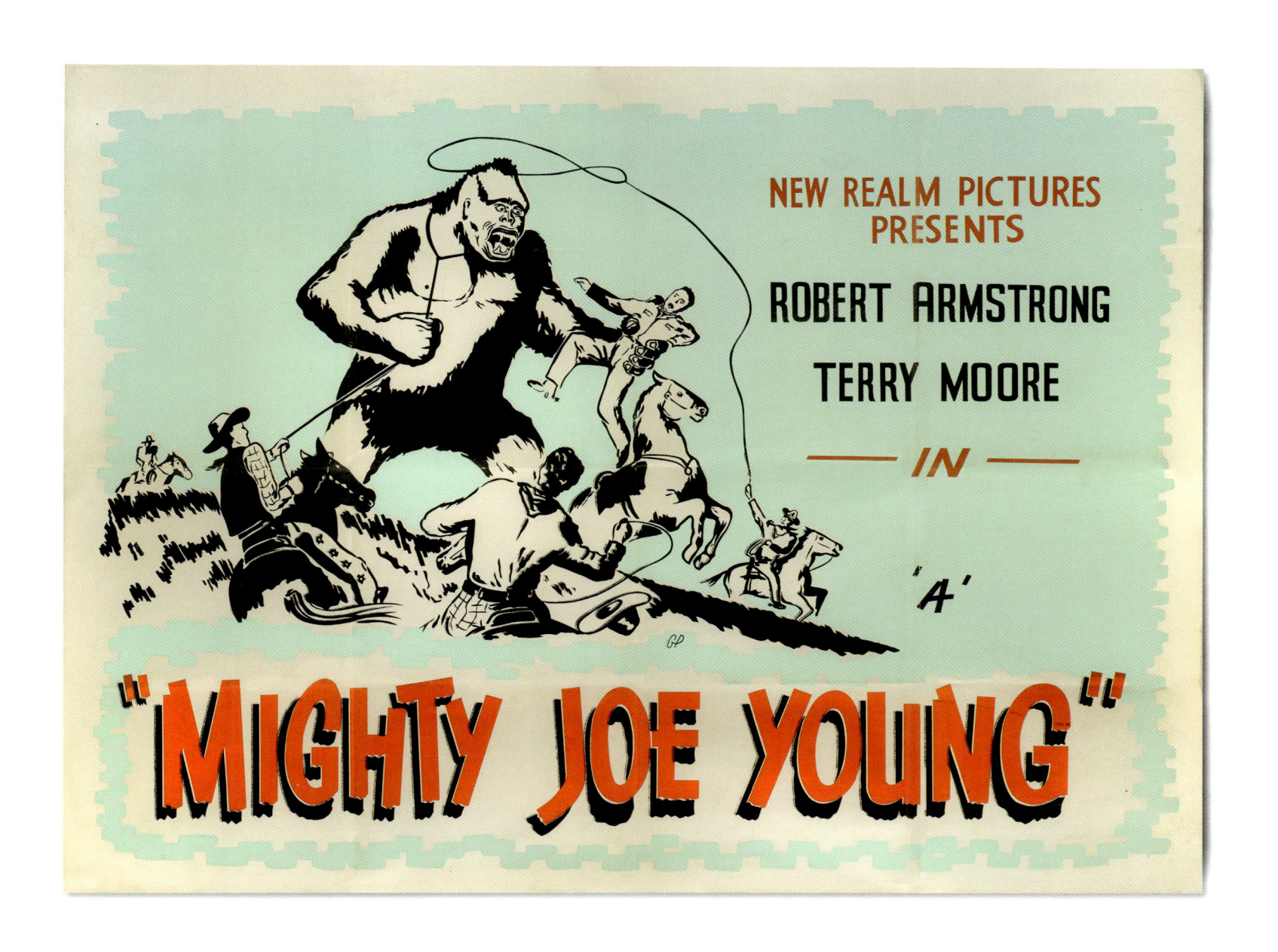

STRIKING! STARTLING! STAGGERIN

John Ford and Merian C. Cooper
present

MIGHTY JOE YOUNG

A MERIAN COOPER'S AMAZING ADVENTURE IN THE UNUSUAL!

starring

TERRY MOORE • BEN JOHNSON

and **ROBERT ARMSTRONG** with **FRANK McHUGH**

Directed by **ERNEST B. SCHOEDSACK**

Technical Creator Willis O'Brien • Screen Play by Ruth Rose

An Arko Production • Distributed by RKO Radio Pictures

PREVIOUS SPREAD: PAGE 22 Italian Fogli (99 x 140cm)
PAGE 23 (Top) British Quad (76 x 102cm) Courtesy of Neil Pettigrew Archive.
(Bottom) US Window Card (36 x 56cm).

THIS SPREAD: (Left) British Quad (76 x 102cm) Courtesy of
Neil Pettigrew Archive. (Above) British (51 x 76cm) Art by Greta Speechly.
Courtesy of Neil Pettigrew Archive.

CHAPTER ONE **MIGHTY JOE YOUNG**

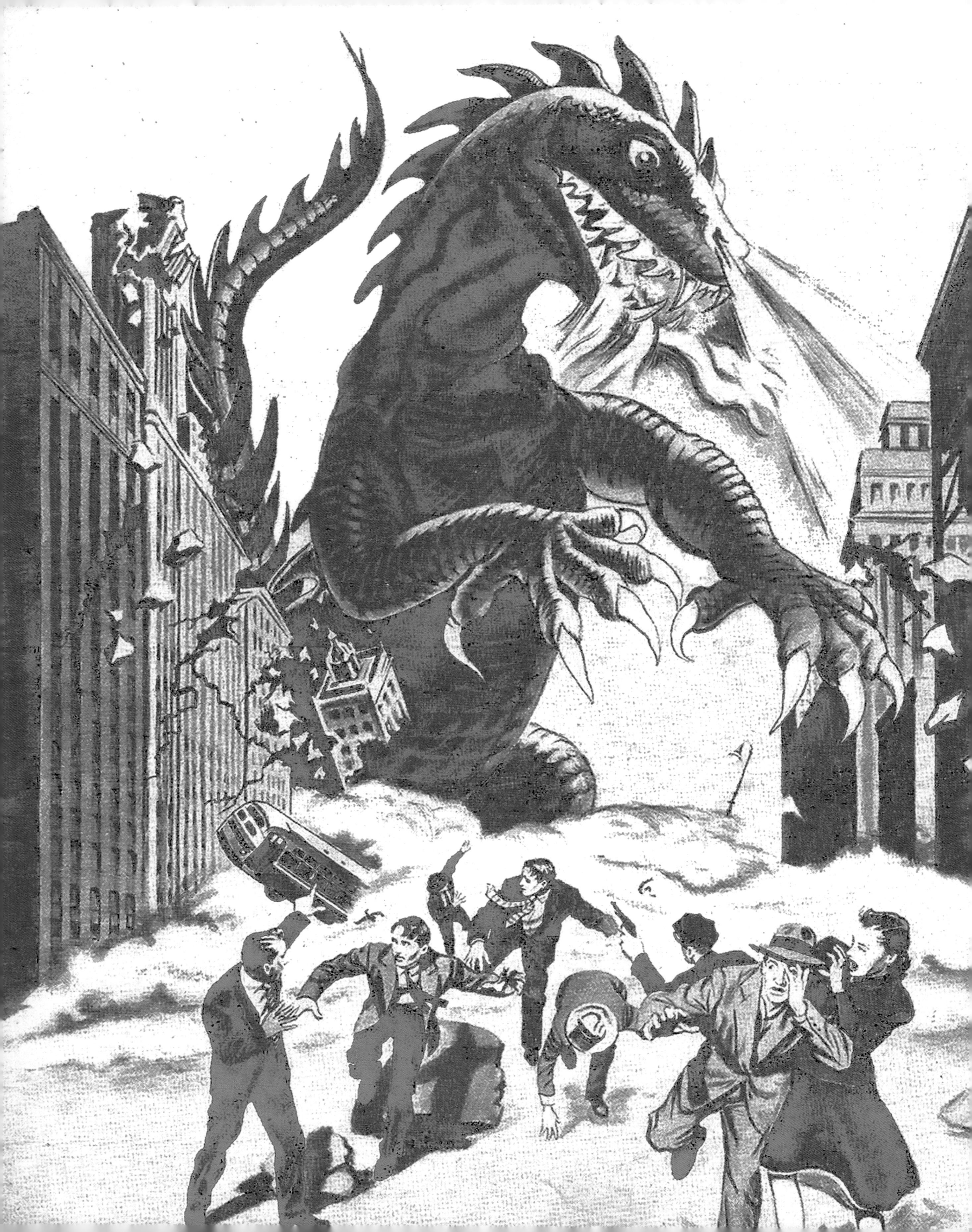

CHAPTER TWO

THE BEAST FROM 20,000 FATHOMS (1953)

TECHNICAL EFFECTS: RAY HARRYHAUSEN

When an atomic test in the Arctic thaws out a 140-million-year-old dinosaur called a Rhedosaurus, the giant beast goes on the rampage. Professor Nesbitt, who witnessed the creature's awakening, and Professor Elson, a paleontologist, warn the authorities that the monster's primeval instinct to survive is driving it towards a network of subterranean caverns off the New York coast. When the Rhedosaurus surfaces in the East River, it clambers ashore, leaving a path of destruction in its wake. Trapped by the military between the burning pillars of the Coney Island rollercoaster, a marksman destroys the beast by shooting it with a deadly radioactive isotope.

KING OF PREHISTORIC SEA GIANTS!

After completing *Mighty Joe Young*, Ray approached a number of major Hollywood studios with ideas for new feature-length films. One of these was *Valley of the Mist* (in partnership with Willis O'Brien), for which he had prepared some detailed drawings of prehistoric animals, and a stop-motion version of H.G. Wells' 1898 science fiction novel *The War of the Worlds*. For the latter project, Ray produced a 16mm test film showing a grotesque Martian emerging from its crashed cylinder, together with twelve drawings of the aliens' terrifying tripod machines laying waste to the cities of Earth. He even discussed the project with his former employer, producer George Pal, who was now working at Paramount Pictures. Sadly the concept never reached fruition, although Pal did eventually turn the book into an Oscar-winning film in 1953, in which he updated Wells' Victorian storyline to the present day.

The problem with stop-motion animation was that the majority of the big Hollywood studios considered the process far too expensive, let alone understood the principles involved. So Ray returned to his work on the short films he was making until he heard that producer Jack Dietz, head of Mutual Films, was scripting a project called *The Monster From Under the Sea*. A simple idea, it concerned a gigantic monster on the rampage in New York, having been brutally awakened from its eons-old slumber by the 1950s' most popular boogeyman, the atom bomb.

THIS PAGE: (Above) Associated British Cinema's marketing for the film included a giant float. (Below) The American artwork for the film was also used for the Mexican release.

HARRYHAUSEN THE MOVIE POSTERS

Ray met with Dietz, the film's director Eugene Lourie (*Gorgo*), and producer Hal E. Chester (*Night of the Demon*), only to discover that the entire budget was a miniscule 150,000 dollars. The amount reserved for the special effects was even more pitiful, totaling a mere 15,000 dollars. But a job was a job, and to his credit, Ray managed to convince them that he could deliver the required stop-motion effects, including the 'monster', well within budget.

While scriptwriters Lou Morheim (*The Outer Limits*) and Fred Freiberger (*Star Trek*) worked on the final screenplay, Ray set about designing and constructing the creature. After some weeks of trial and error, he settled on a dinosaur hybrid. Ray's father, Fred, machined the ball-and-socket armature (the flexible endoskeleton), which Ray covered with a cotton-padded framework of sponge rubber muscles and latex skin, textured to resemble alligator hide. A seven-inch puppet of the head and neck section was also made for close-ups.

Ray began work on the stop-motion effects in August 1952, first making some test shots in his home studio to ensure that the split-screen technique (used to great effect in *Mighty Joe Young*) to combine an animated model with live-action background plates would work. He then spent the next five months animating the Rhedosaurus (as the fictional animal was now called) and its various encounters with an atomic explosion, Arctic ice flows, ships at sea, an isolated lighthouse, and the canyon-like streets of New York City. To save money, photographic enlargements (instead of the more expensive filmed back-projection plates) were made of several buildings in Manhattan and placed directly behind the stop-motion model on the animation tabletop.

A lot of the film is taken up with the Rhedosaurus prowling the streets of New York (much like King Kong had done back in 1933), while panic-stricken members of the public flee for their lives. For the climax of the picture, the dinosaur is cornered by the army and meets its demise within the towering steel latticework of the famous Coney Island scenic railway.

The film was retitled *The Beast From 20,000 Fathoms* thanks to a short story by Ray's lifelong friend, fellow dinosaur enthusiast and science fiction author Ray Bradbury, which had been published in the *Saturday Evening Post* magazine. Bradbury's story (also known as *The Foghorn*) relates how a lonely dinosaur mistakes the sound of a lighthouse siren for a mating call. This idea was also used to great effect in the finished film.

With the exception of Cecil Kellaway (*I Married a Witch*) as paleontologist Professor Thurgood Elson, and Kenneth Tobey (*The Thing*) as the army officer in charge of stopping the beast, the cast was relatively unknown. Swiss actor Paul Christian played the hero Professor Tom Nesbitt, and newcomer Paula Raymond was cast as the heroine, Lee Hunter.

With cinema exhibition changing in the early 1950s and the emergence of both 3-D and widescreen, Dietz was fearful that his black and white movie couldn't compete with the latest cinema fads, so he sold it outright to Warner Brothers for 400,000 dollars. Warners decided to advertise the film with the byline 'Glorious Sepia Tone', and released it with tinted sequences. It opened in America in June 1953, on a double-bill with a film about the Civil War called *Kansas Pacific*.

Thanks to a very impressive publicity campaign, with full-color poster art of the beast towering over the New York skyline, the film brought in a hefty profit of five million dollars. The studio's marketing department even 'borrowed' actor Colin Clive's immortal line from the original 1931 film version of *Frankenstein* by placing a word balloon on the posters announcing, 'It's alive!'.

Having received tremendous feedback regarding the foyer promotion for its 3D movie *House of Wax* (1953), Warner Brothers also produced a ten-foot-high display board for *The Beast From 20,000 Fathoms*, with a hidden motor that made the Rhedosaurus's eye move and its tongue flick in and out. Costing a miniscule sixteen dollars to hire, this ambitious advertising tool was credited in the campaign book as 'The first and only animated front-of-house accessory ever created by a motion picture company.'

While the majority of the film posters that accompanied the film worldwide copied the stunning American artwork, there were one or two notable exceptions. Italian artist Luigi Martinati painted a glowing image of the beast towering over a battalion of soldiers (*Il risveglio del dinosauro*), while Belgian artist Wik opted for the climax of the film on Coney Island (*Le Monstre Des Temps Perdus*).

Although it was promoted in America as a children's film, the Australian market declared it unsuitable for youngsters. In a (not so rare) moment of pure lunacy, the British Board of Film Censors agreed with that verdict and slapped an X certificate (no admittance under the age of sixteen) on the film. Shortly after completing a smash-hit run in September 1953 at the London Pavilion in Piccadilly Circus, *The Beast From 20,000 Fathoms* was released on the ABC (Associated British Cinemas) circuit in October, with an early Hammer movie called *The Flanagan Boy*.

The critics were pretty unanimous in their praise for the film, labeling it in hindsight as the first of the atomic-age monster movies. A few years later, the Japanese director Ishiro Hondo credited the movie as the inspiration for *Godzilla*. Although shown on American television in the late 1950s, British audiences had to wait until 1967 before it made an appearance on commercial television.

THIS PAGE: (Above) Warner Brother's animated lobby display for *The Beast From 20,000 Fathoms*.

> The film was labeled the first of the atomic-age monster movies.

CHAPTER TWO **THE BEAST FROM 20,000 FATHOMS**

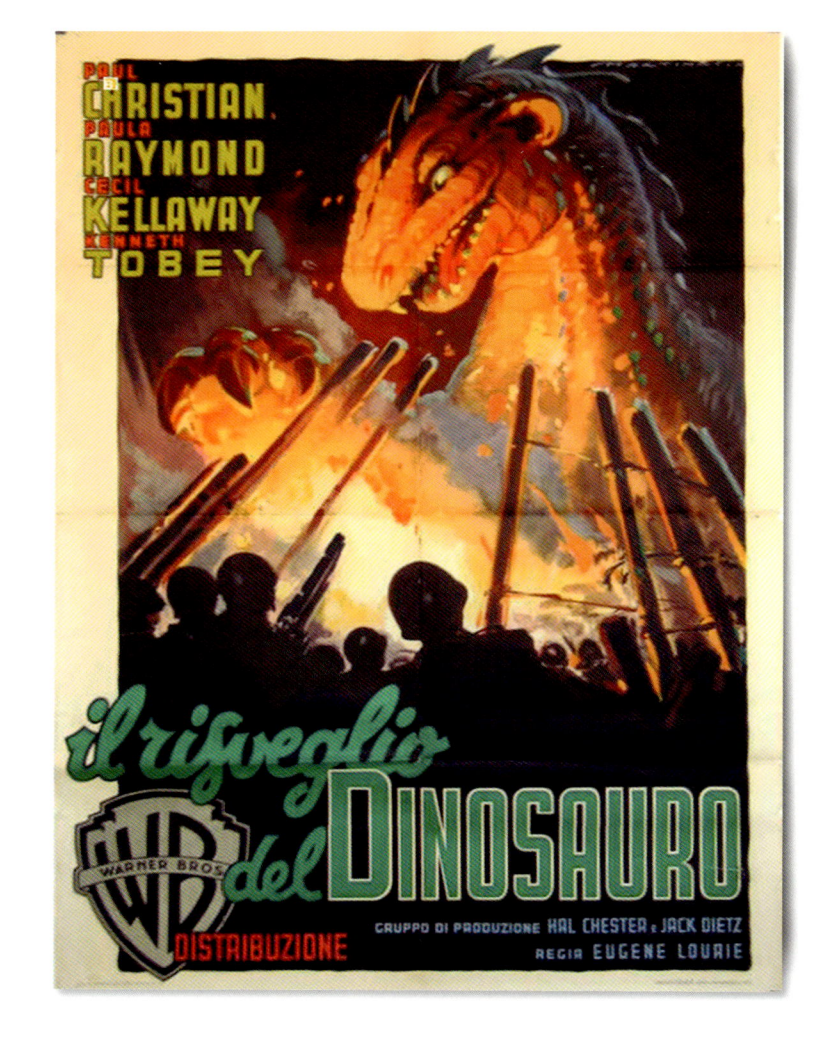

HARRYHAUSEN THE MOVIE POSTERS

CHAPTER TWO **THE BEAST FROM 20,000 FATHOMS**

HARRYHAUSEN THE MOVIE POSTERS

PREVIOUS SPREAD: PAGE 30 (Left) US Insert (36 x 91cm) (Top Right) Italian Fogli (99 x 104cm) Art by Luigi Martinati. (Bottom Right) French (58 x 76cm). PAGE 31 US Teaser One-sheet (101 x 152cm).

THIS SPREAD: (Left) British Quad (76 x 102cm). (Above) Belgian (36 x 48cm) Art by Wik. Courtesy of Mike Hankin Archive.

CHAPTER TWO **THE BEAST FROM 20,000 FATHOMS**

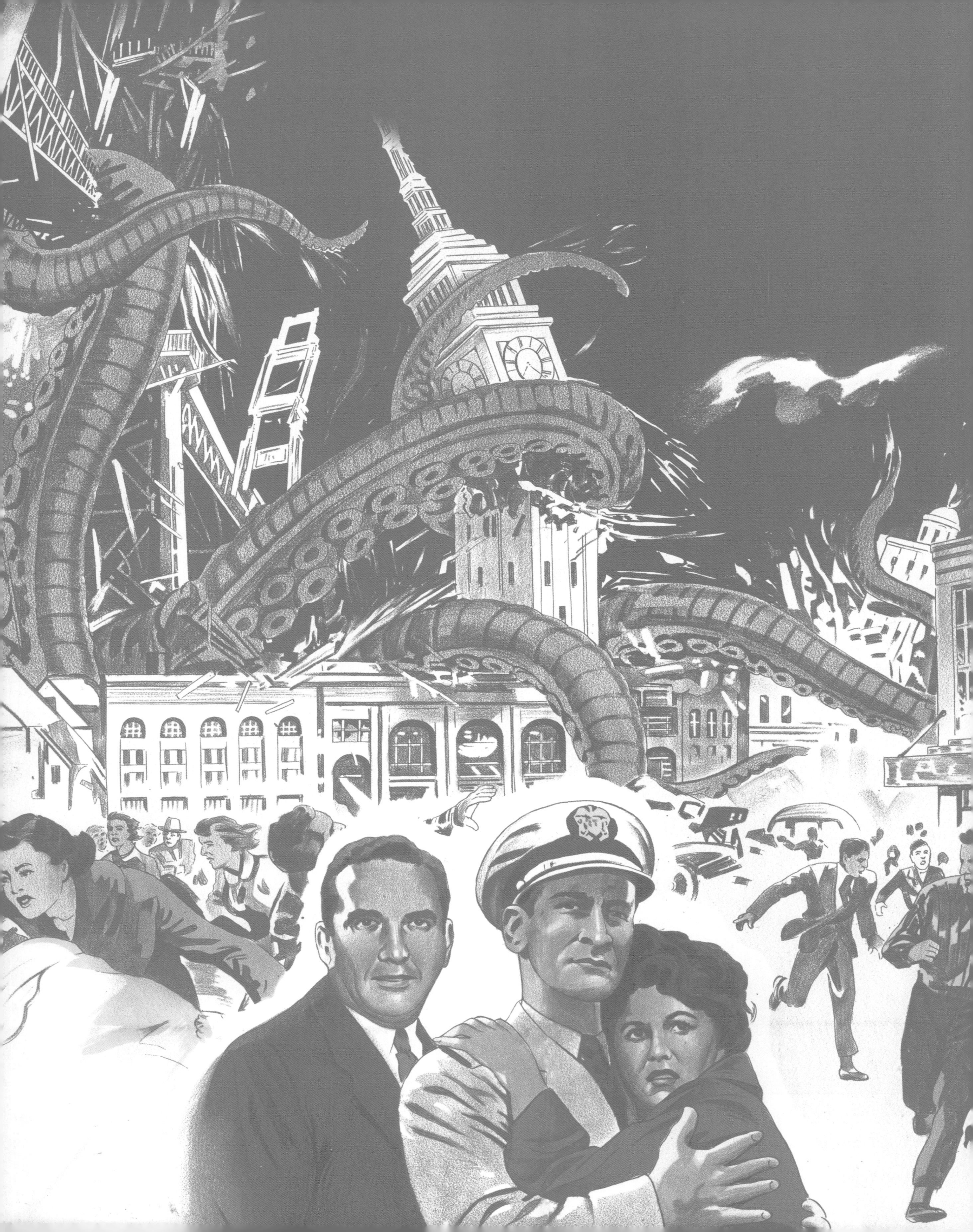

CHAPTER THREE

IT CAME FROM BENEATH THE SEA (1955)

TECHNICAL EFFECTS: RAY HARRYHAUSEN

The residual radiation from an H-Bomb test in the Pacific Ocean transforms a giant octopus into an unstoppable monster. After attacking a cargo ship at sea, the creature's movements are kept under close surveillance by two scientists: Dr. John Carter, an analytical biologist, and Professor Leslie Joyce, an expert in marine life. By order of the Defense Department, the entire Eastern Seaboard is put on high alert after the octopus emerges from the ocean and attacks the city of San Francisco, toppling the Golden Gate Bridge and a number of waterfront buildings. Forced back into the water by flamethrowers, the creature is finally destroyed by a harpoon fired into its central nervous system.

A TIDAL WAVE OF TERROR!

After *The Beast From 20,000 Fathoms*, Ray once again considered resurrecting some of his older projects. He even toyed with an idea of making a feature film about Sinbad the Sailor from the *Arabian Nights*. But then word came of a young producer, Charles Hirsh Schneer, who was so impressed by the box office success of *The Beast From 20,000 Fathoms* that he wanted to make his own monster picture.

Schneer, who worked for the legendary Sam Katzman at Columbia Pictures, had already developed a reputation for making credible B-movies on almost non-existent budgets. Schneer wanted his monster to be a giant radioactive octopus that attacks San Francisco. While this might seem a rather corny idea, it should be remembered that the year was 1954 and Hollywood, obsessed with the science fiction genre, was busy financing numerous movies about giant creatures and atomic mutations.

Ray met with Schneer and was delighted that the latter wanted to use stop-motion for the film's cephalopod star. The two men also struck up a working relationship that would eventually lead to a three-picture deal with Columbia, followed by a lifetime of making movies together.

While Ray produced some storyboard sketches of how he thought the special effects scenes could be accomplished, Schneer assigned scriptwriters George Worthington Yates (*Them!*) and Hal Smith (*The Defiant Ones*) to write the screenplay. Robert Gordon (*Black Zoo*) was chosen to direct the film, now retitled *It Came From Beneath the Sea*.

THIS PAGE: (Above) San Francisco falls prey to Ray's stop-motion octopus. (Below) This colorful American lobby card captures the moment when the giant octopus attacks the Golden Gate Bridge.

HARRYHAUSEN THE MOVIE POSTERS

The stars of the film included Faith Domergue (*This Island Earth*), Kenneth Tobey (*The Beast From 20,000 Fathoms*), and Donald Curtis (*The Ten Commandments*). Hundreds of extras were paid to run around during the octopus attack, and though permission was granted by the San Francisco City Fathers to film in the Bay Area, they objected to any proposal that would show the magnificent Golden Gate Bridge being destroyed by a giant sea beast. So sections of the bridge had to be shot in secret in order for Ray to later combine them with a miniature version of the structure. The highlight of the film is most definitely the moment when the towering pylons and carriageway are crushed by the octopus' powerful tentacles.

Location footage, miniatures, split-screen and rear projection were used to combine the live-action footage with Ray's stop-motion effects. Because the film's budget was so tight (150,000 dollars), Ray had to save money by constructing a six-tentacled octopus (which he called a 'sixtopus') over an armature made by his father. This required less animation and less time to shoot, but the master animator cleverly disguised the fact that his monstrous sea creature was missing two limbs by always keeping part of it under the water.

Considering the low budget and the limitations of an octopus as a main character — even a colossal specimen — the film features some fine special effects utilizing Ray's customized rear-projection and split-screen system. The creature's nighttime attack on the Canadian freighter is extremely effective, with shots of the tentacles rising into the air behind the doomed ship. This, and the sequence in which the octopus crushes the famous Embarcadero clock tower on the Oakland Ferry Building, became the main selling point on the posters.

It Came From Beneath the Sea opened in America in June 1955, and was released nationwide a month later. While the budget might have suggested a B-movie status, the film was promoted as the main feature on a double-bill with the low-budget *Creature With the Atom Brain*. It performed very strongly in most territories and received positive feedback from the critics. The following month it opened nationwide in the UK with an A certificate. It was never re-issued in either America or Britain, and UK television audiences had to wait until 1974 for its debut screening on the commercial channel.

Although the bulk of film poster art relied on the image of the tentacles crushing the clock tower and the Golden Gate Bridge, European poster art explored different aspects of the production. In Italy, artist and former set designer Alfredo Capitani (1895–1985) painted an impressive image of the film's two stars (Tobey and Domergue) and the octopus sinking the sea freighter (*Le Mostro dei Mari*). The British two-tone quad poster opted for a black and white photographic montage, but also illustrated the octopus attacking the San Francisco docks and sinking the ship.

> The film utilized Ray's customized rear-projection and split-screen system.

THIS PAGE: (Top) An ambitious marquee display at the Essoldo Cinema in Hackney, East London. (Left) The cover of the American double feature Campaign Book.

CHAPTER THREE **IT CAME FROM BENEATH THE SEA**

HARRYHAUSEN THE MOVIE POSTERS

CHAPTER THREE **IT CAME FROM BENEATH THE SEA**

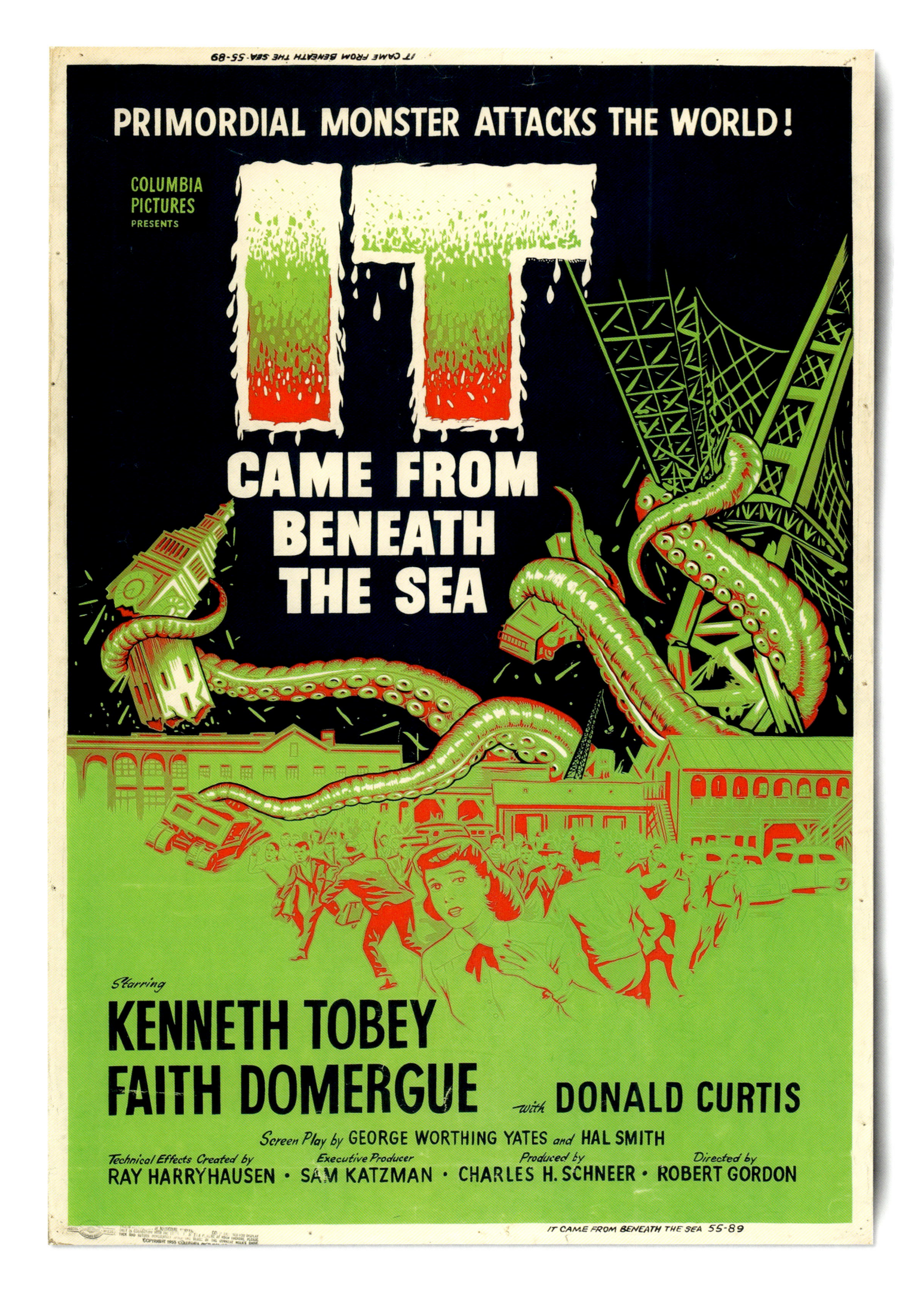

HARRYHAUSEN THE MOVIE POSTERS

PREVIOUS SPREAD: PAGE 38 US One-sheet (69 x 104cm) Courtesy of Ray Harryhausen Archive. PAGE 39 US silk-screen (101 x 152cm).

THIS SPREAD: (Far Left) Italian Fogli (139 x 198cm) Art by Alfredo Capitani. Courtesy of Neil Pettigrew Archive. (Left) US Insert (36 x 91cm) Courtesy of Neil Pettigrew Archive. (Above) Belgian (36 x 48cm) Courtesy of Mike Hankin Archive.

CHAPTER THREE **IT CAME FROM BENEATH THE SEA**

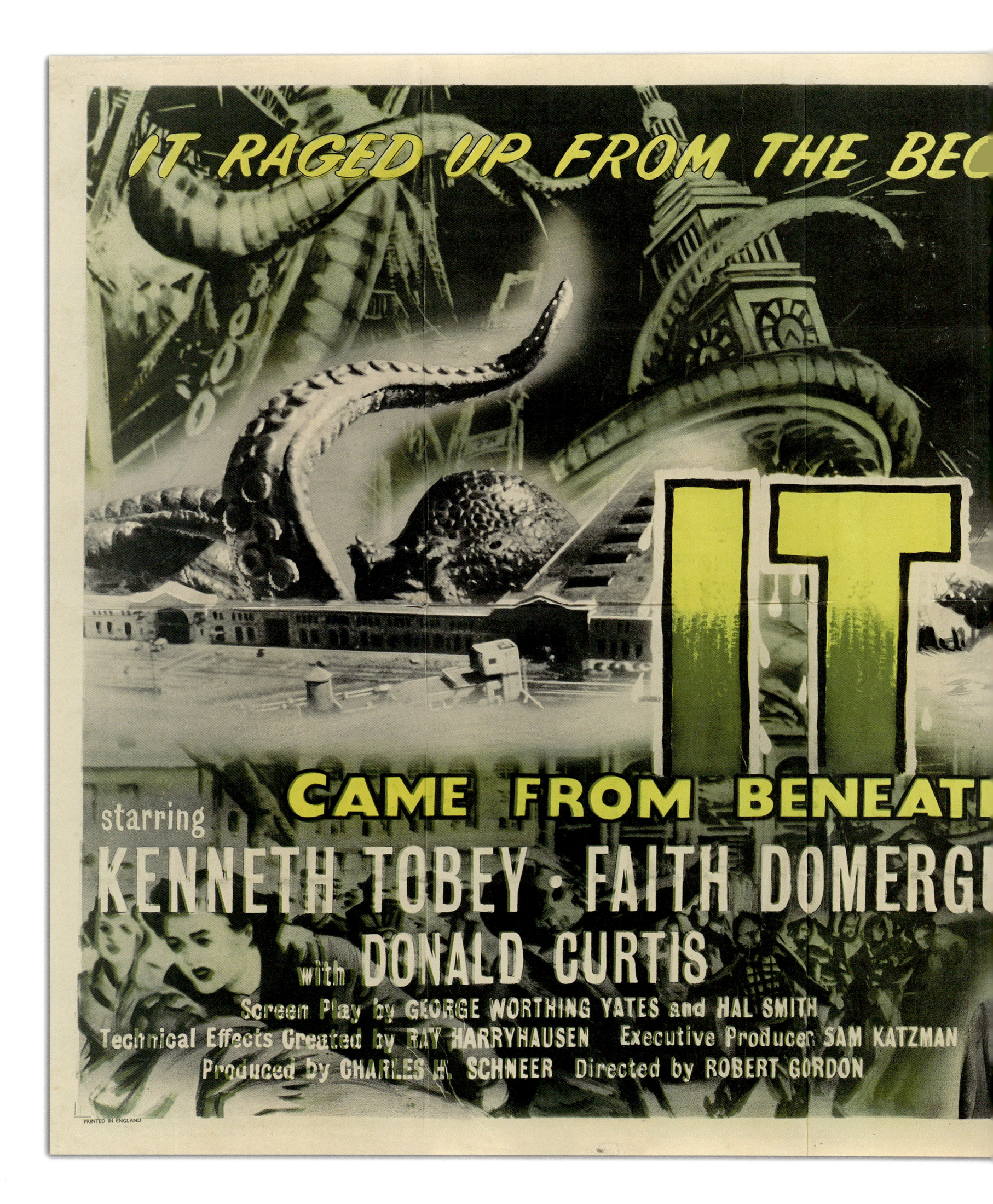

HARRYHAUSEN THE MOVIE POSTERS

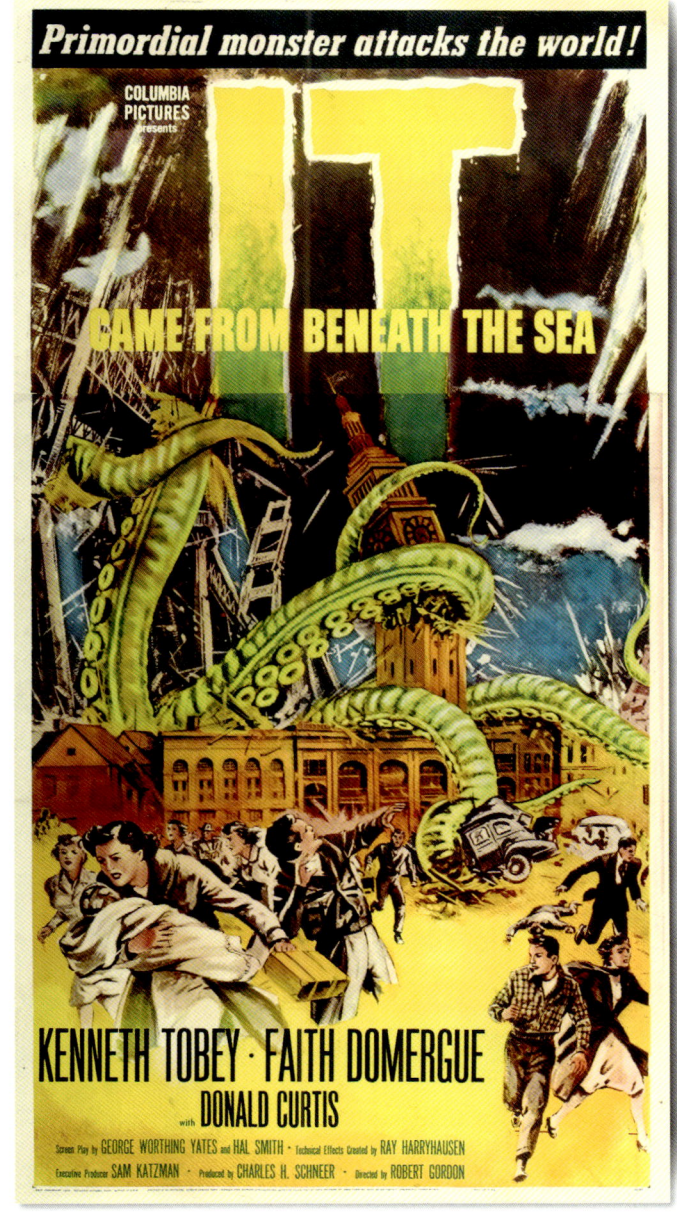

THIS SPREAD: (Left) British Quad (76 x 102cm) Courtesy of Simon Greetham Archive. (Above) US Three-sheet (104 x 206cm).

CHAPTER THREE **IT CAME FROM BENEATH THE SEA** 43

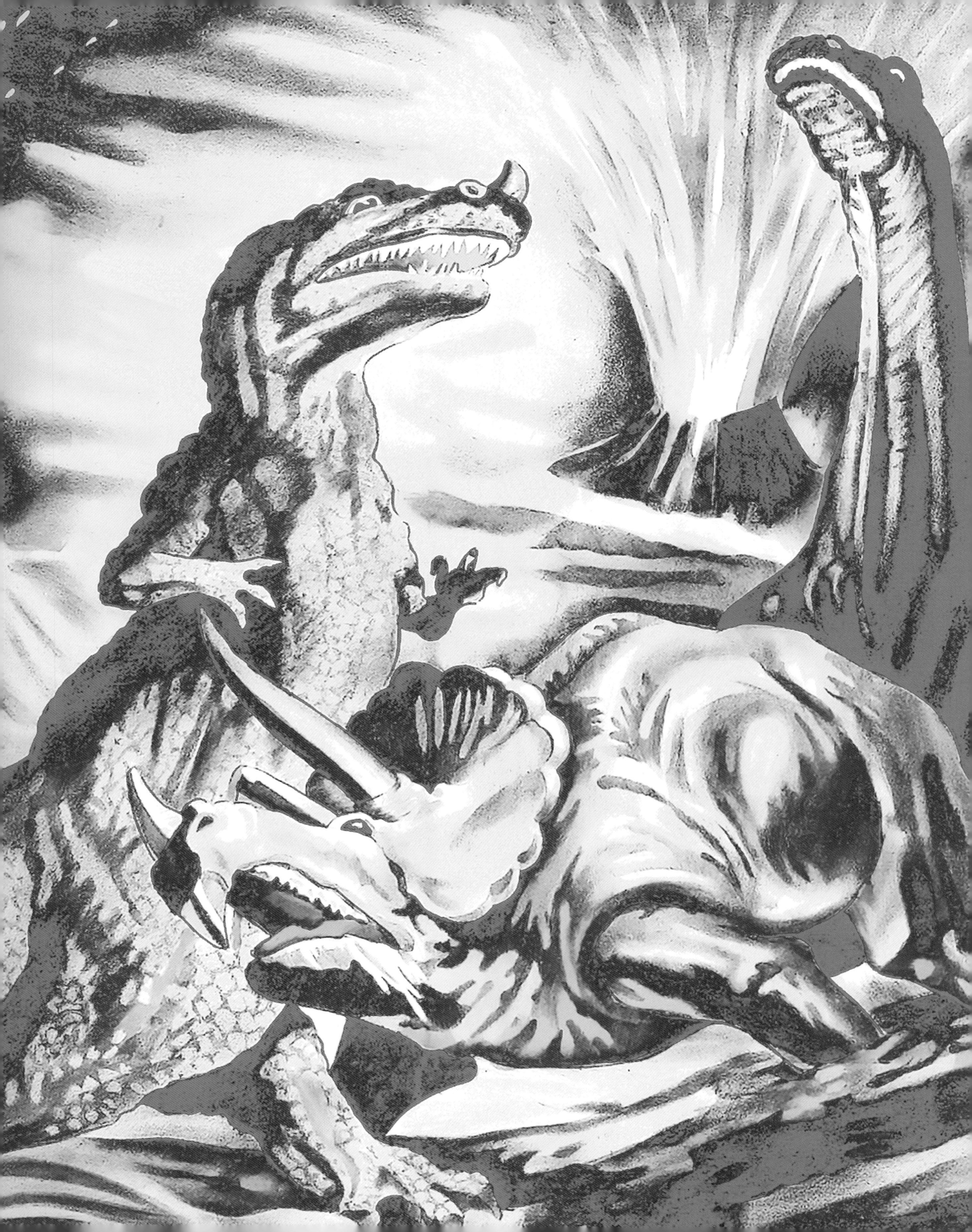

CHAPTER FOUR

THE ANIMAL WORLD (1956)

ANIMATION: RAY HARRYHAUSEN

A wildlife documentary that goes behind the scenes on the wonders of the animal kingdom, from the age of the dinosaurs to the present day. Against a backdrop of lush jungle foliage, giant prehistoric beasts battle with each other for survival. In a cataclysmic finale, the huge creatures are wiped out by a massive earthquake and an erupting volcano.

2 BILLION YEARS IN THE MAKING!

The prehistoric denizens of King Kong's Skull Island home had enthralled Ray Harryhausen from the moment he first saw the classic monster movie in 1933. Already a huge dinosaur fan and a great admirer of the paleoart of sculptor and artist Charles R. Knight, whose models and paintings have inspired so many filmmakers over the years, from Willis O'Brien's silent version of *The Lost World* (1925) to 'The Rite of Spring' sequence in Walt Disney's *Fantasia* (1940), it was always inevitable that Ray's early experiments with stop-motion would include such creatures. He even planned an ambitious project called *Evolution* about the beginnings of life on Earth. Having prepared some extraordinarily evocative art for the film, as well as constructing miniature sets and extremely detailed latex models, he shelved the idea when *Fantasia* opened, feeling that the film's spectacular dinosaur sequence had made his own project irrelevant.

Although the first feature film on which he had sole credit for the stop-motion work (*The Beast From 20,000 Fathoms*) had included a prehistoric animal with T-Rex-like jaws and a row of dragon-sized plates along its back, it was purely an invention of Ray's imagination. Recreating authentic-looking dinosaurs based on the latest scientific facts seemed a distant hope, when suddenly out of the blue he received a telephone call from Willis O'Brien. The year was 1955 and Ray had been busy working on preliminary storyboards for his second film with Charles Schneer about flying saucers, but delays in the production enabled him to moonlight with O'Brien's production team on *The Animal World*, a documentary about life on Earth that producer Irwin Allen was filming for Warner Brothers.

Allen (who later went on to produce some of the most successful science fiction television series of the 1960s: *Voyage to the Bottom of the Sea*, *Lost in Space*, *The Time Tunnel* and *Land of the Giants*, as well as 70s blockbusters *The Poseidon Adventure* and *The Towering Inferno*) had already made an Oscar-winning documentary about the oceans called *The Sea Around Us* (1952). Successful at the box office, its sole purpose had been to cash in on Walt Disney's award-winning *True-Life Adventures* series.

For *The Animal World* Allen had employed O'Brien to supervise a brand new stop-motion sequence, with Ray contracted to handle the more laborious work of animating the prehistoric creatures. To save money (as the dinosaur sequence would be the most costly part of the film) Allen even considered purchasing footage from Ray's *Evolution* film, but the idea was shelved.

In order to make the dinosaurs in the film as authentic as possible Allen hired Charles L. Camp, Professor of Paleontology at the University of California, to work alongside O'Brien. Members of a special effects team, who also made larger mechanical versions of the animals for close-ups, carried out the sculpting of the creatures and the construction of the miniature dioramas in which they lived out their violent existence.

A section of one of the Warner Brothers sound stages was fenced off for the animation work, and the shooting of the models took well over three months to complete. But at least there was no need for complicated post-production work involving split-screen or live action footage, as the entire dinosaur sequence was shot using just the stop-motion models and painted backdrops. Two cameras were utilised to capture as much footage as possible, and lasting approximately ten minutes the sequence is undoubtedly the highlight of the film. The Warner Brothers' publicity department must have felt the same way, as the film's extensive publicity focuses almost entirely on the prehistoric animals.

The *Animal World* was press-screened in America in December 1955, in the hope that it might win Warner Brothers another Academy Award for Best Documentary. Sadly, it wasn't even nominated. A general release in America followed in June 1956. Six months later, on December 17th 1956, it opened in the UK, but was relegated to second billing on the ABC cinema circuit with a British 'science fiction' film called *Satellite in the Sky*. Industry magazine *Kinematograph Weekly*, however, reported that the 'double-bill' fared better at the box-office than all the competition put together.

Ray was somewhat bemused and no doubt greatly flattered by the fact that the dinosaurs became the film's main selling point, dominating the advertising campaign in both America and Britain. With the byline '2 Billion Years in the Making', the stunning poster artwork by Gustav Rehberger features a ceratosaurus being impaled in the stomach by the horn of a charging triceratops, while a brontosaurus, like a reluctant spectator to the battle, screeches its defiance against a stark image of an exploding volcano. American company Sawyers produced a three-reel, View-master set with 3D scenes from the dinosaur sequence called *Battle of the Monsters*, and Western Publishing printed a tie-in Dell comic book.

Interestingly, one or two of the European posters for the film do include the dinosaurs in redrawn versions of the American publicity campaign, but concentrate instead on the modern animals that make up the other seven-eighths of the film's total screen time. Artist Luigi Martinati's stylish Italian poster for the film (*Mondo Meraviglioso*), features an antelope, surprisingly unfazed by the titanic prehistoric battle going on in the background. The Belgium poster by ITK (*Le Monde Des Animaux*), on the other hand, places the battling saurians within a framework of assorted jungle creatures.

THIS PAGE: (Above) A tyrannosaurus and a triceratops battle for survival thanks to the genius of stop-motion animation.

HARRYHAUSEN THE MOVIE POSTERS

CHAPTER FOUR **THE ANIMAL WORLD**

HARRYHAUSEN THE MOVIE POSTERS

PREVIOUS PAGE: PAGE 47 (Top Left) US One-sheet (69 x 104cm) Art by Gustav Rehberger. (Bottom Left) Belgian (36 x 48cm) Courtesy of Mike Hankin Archive. (Right) US Insert (36 x 91cm) Art by Gustav Rehberger. Courtesy of Ray Harryhausen Archive.

THIS SPREAD: (Left) US Half-sheet (56 x 71cm) Art by Gustav Rehberger. (Above) Italian Foglio (71 x 99cm).

CHAPTER FOUR **THE ANIMAL WORLD**

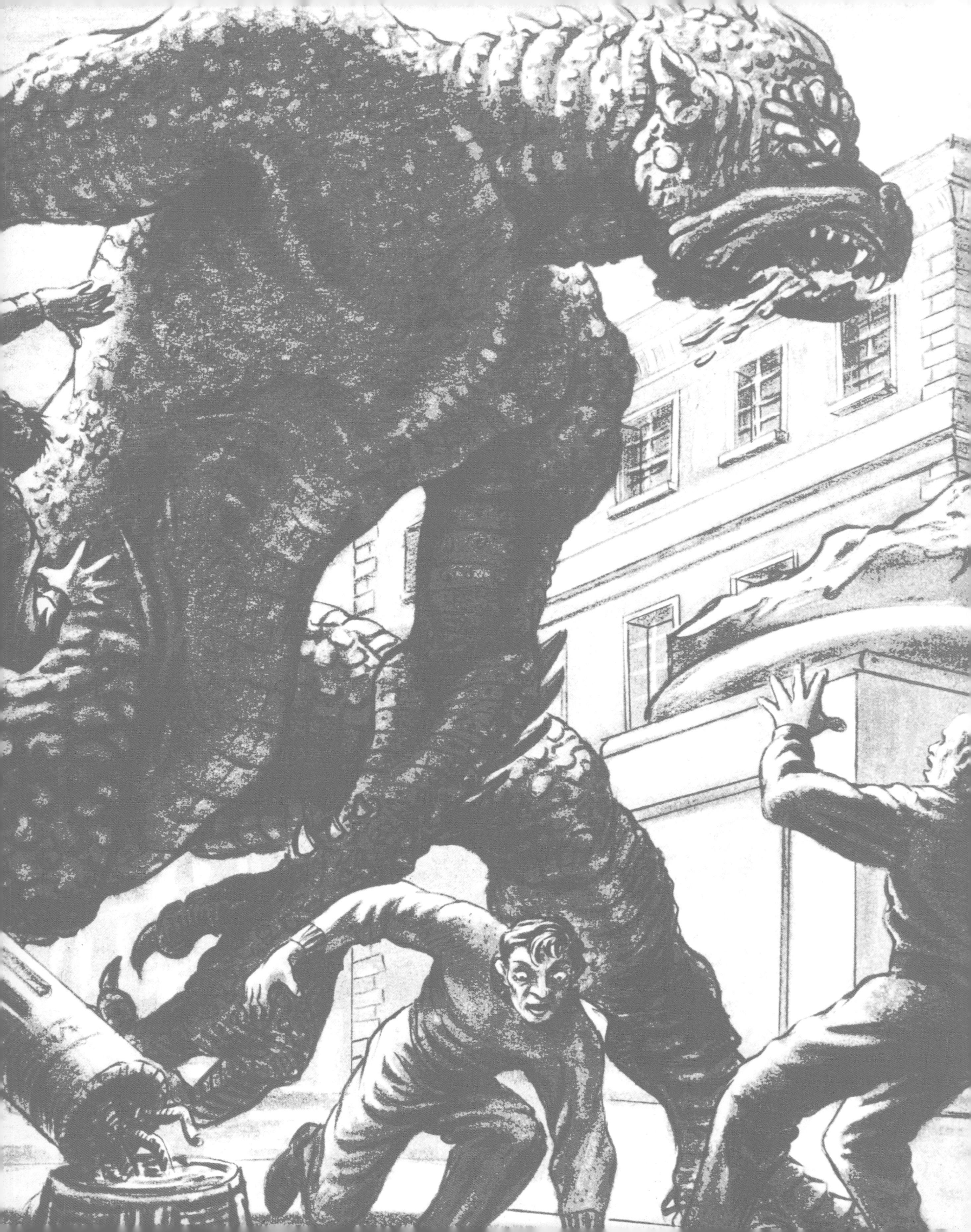

CHAPTER FIVE

EARTH VS. THE FLYING SAUCERS (1956) 20 MILLION MILES TO EARTH (1957)

TECHNICAL EFFECTS: RAY HARRYHAUSEN

EARTH VS. THE FLYING SAUCERS: A top-secret missile program called 'Operation Skyhook' is sabotaged when its missiles are shot down by flying saucers. Scientist Russ Marvin decides to meet the invaders in order to ward off the risk of an interplanetary war. Kidnapped by the aliens, Marvin and his wife are given just fifty-six days to persuade the nations of the Earth to surrender the planet or face total annihilation. As the flying saucers rain down fire and destruction on Washington D.C., the scientists invent a high-frequency retaliatory weapon to stop the invasion.

20 MILLION MILES TO EARTH: A rocket returning to Earth from the planet Venus crashes into the sea off the coast of Sicily. Rescuing two of the crew, the authorities are unaware that a strange egg-shaped object has also been washed ashore. Coming to the attention of zoologist Dr. Leonardo and his daughter Marisa, the 'alien egg' hatches into a 38cm-high Venusian creature called an Ymir, which has three talons and a human-like torso. Within a very short space of time the creature has doubled in size, and continues to grow. After reaching six meters in height, the Ymir terrorizes the citizens of Rome before taking refuge inside the walls of the Colosseum, where the army finally kills it.

ATTENTION EARTH-PEOPLE!
EARTH VS. THE FLYING SAUCERS

Ray's second major project for Schneer and Columbia, *Earth Vs. the Flying Saucers* was one of his most unusual, although the fact that he'd once planned a stop-motion version of H.G. Wells' *The War of the Worlds* meant it was not too surprising. The idea for the film actually started with Schneer, who was aware of the public's growing interest in space exploration and flying saucers. Ray was equally excited about the project, seeing it as a departure from the sort of creature-led special effects that he'd been involved with before.

Working closely with writer Curt Siodmak (*Frankenstein Meets the Wolfman*) and then George Worthington Yates (*It Came From Beneath the Sea*), Ray produced an extensive visual interpretation of the script, which was based on Major Donald E. Keyhoe's bestseller *Flying Saucers From Outer Space*. Scriptwriter Bernard Gordon (*The Day of the Triffids*) was brought in by Schneer to complete the task, although his final screen credit was under the pseudonym Raymond T. Marcus.

Ray used photographs of famous landmarks in Washington D.C. (the aliens' beachhead) and combined them with images of the invading saucers, in order to indicate how the scenes would appear in the final movie. He also contacted many people who claimed to have met extraterrestrials. Location filming was conducted at a wastewater

THIS PAGE: (Above) Not stop-motion models, the aliens were played by actors. (Below) A strip cartoon version of the story to promote the film in newspapers and periodicals.

treatment plant in Los Angles, which doubled as the film's fictional headquarters. The unusual sound made by the plant's disintegration tanks was also recorded during filming and later used as the whirring sound of the alien ships.

On Ray's instructions, his father built three aluminum model saucers in various sizes from three inches to a single twelve-inch version for close-ups and an 18-inch version made of wood. The aliens themselves (creatures that were encased in faceless robot-like space suits) were all played by actors, as budgetary restrictions didn't allow for the use of stop-motion figures. But Ray wasn't sorry, given the time it took to animate the flying saucers. To simulate flight, they were suspended on wires, with a technique later referred to as aerial brace work; a process that Ray would use time and again in films such as *Jason and the Argonauts* (1963) and *One Million Years B.C.* (1966). Ray also came up with a brilliant way to give the streamlined saucers a feeling of motion. He constructed the outer rims of the ships independently of the centre section. By adding parallel lines and rotating the sections frame by frame, the moving lines give the illusion that the saucers were spinning as they moved across the sky.

At the climax of the film the saucers collide with some of Washington D.C.'s most iconic buildings, so detailed miniatures costing nearly 3,000 dollars were made of the Capitol Building, the Washington Monument and the Supreme Court. Ray also animated the destruction sequences in stop-motion, pulling the miniature buildings apart brick-by-brick, one frame at a time.

Fighting the deadly invasion of Earth was Hugh Marlowe (*It Came From Outer Space*) as scientist Dr. Russell Marvin, whose job it was to defeat the aliens. Assisting him in his task is his wife Carol (Joan Taylor), with Morris Ankrum (*Rocketship X-M*) playing the hotheaded Brigadier General John Hanley. Former actor Fred F. Sears (*The Giant Claw*) was chosen to direct the film, and veteran voice-over artist Paul Frees (*The War of the Worlds*) provided the alien leader's sinister voice.

The film's amazing special effects, coupled with the nationwide interest in UFOs, proved a godsend to Columbia's publicity department. When the film opened in America in July 1956, on a double-bill with a low-budget horror entitled *The Werewolf*, it was accompanied by some spectacular artwork depicting sinister looking aliens and a sky full of death-ray-spewing flying saucers. The studio's marketing department also mimicked the numerous reports that filled the newspapers and popular periodicals of the time by using exploitative headlines such as 'Flying Saucers Attack', or 'Warning! Take Cover!' These phrases also parodied the government's official broadcasts about the threat of atomic attack, which obsessed the American public during the 1950s.

European publicity for the film was far more imaginative. Italian film poster artist Anselmo Ballester (1897-1974), who illustrated promotional posters for two of Ray's 1950s science fiction films, evokes a tremendous feeling of foreboding with his artwork for *Earth Vs. the Flying Saucers*. One of which shows the film's two stars (Marlowe and Taylor) surrounded by colorful spinning discs designed to represent the alien spacecraft.

The original German poster (*Fliegende Untertassen*), by an unidentified artist, shows Ray's saucers crashing into the skyscrapers of New York. The Belgian poster (*L'Invasion Des Soucoupes Volantes*) was a much cruder design in black and orange, while the Swedish poster (*Anfall Fran Rymden*) by artist V. Lipniunas highlights a damsel-in-distress at the mercy of the robotic aliens.

Earth Vs. the Flying Saucers was distributed in the UK in April 1957, through a small independent company called Eros. Sharing a double-bill with a low-budget western called *The Hostage*, the distributor pulled out all the stops with the publicity, designing not one, but two quad posters. The most striking design is the poster with Joan Taylor looking suitably alarmed as the invaders raze a nameless city to the ground with their death rays. Although never re-released in the UK, the film was finally shown on British television's commercial channel in 1975.

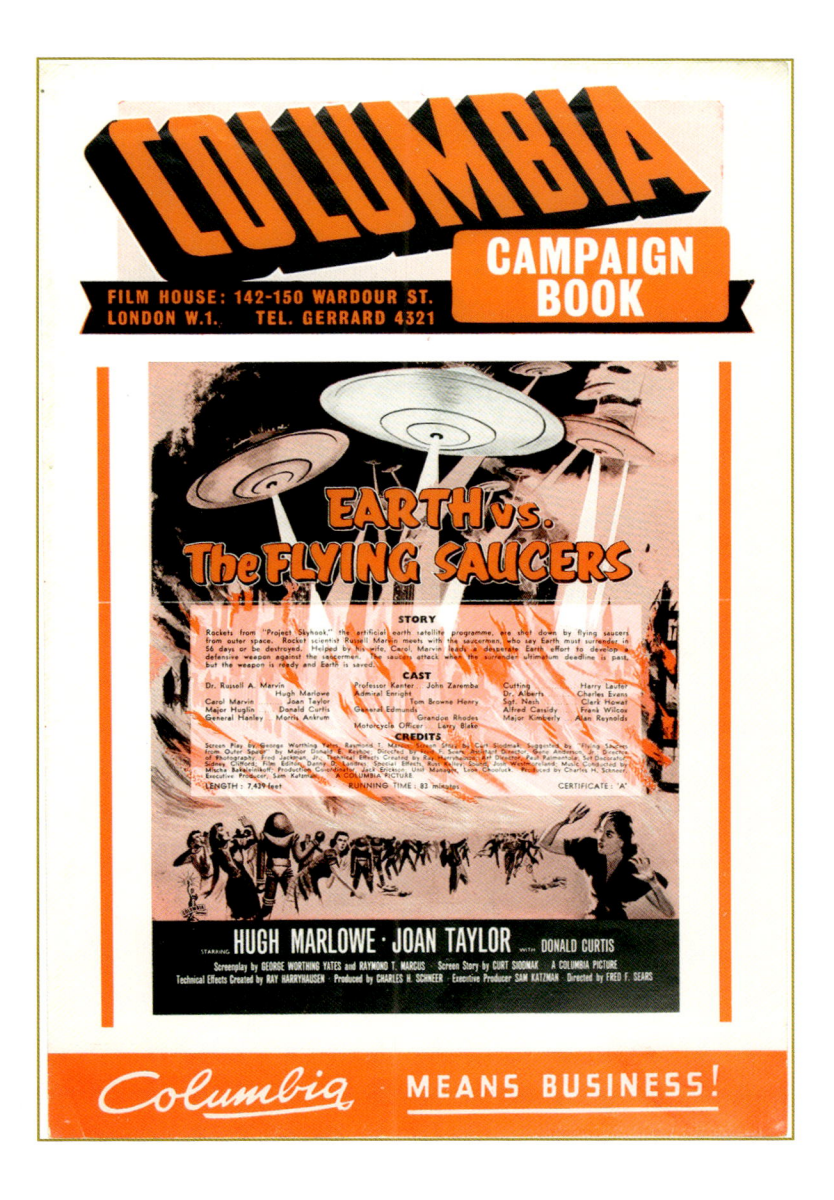

THIS PAGE: (Left) A Mexican lobby card. (Above) Cover for the British Campaign Book that was designed to help cinemas promote the film.

CHAPTER FIVE **EARTH VS THE FLYING SAUCERS**

FLYING SAUCERS ATTACK!
WARNING! TAKE COVER!
FLYING SAUCERS
INVADE OUR PLANET!
WASHINGTON, LONDON,
PARIS, MOSCOW
FIGHT BACK!
EARTH vs. THE FLYING SAUCERS
starring HUGH MARLOWE · JOAN TAYLOR with DONALD CURTIS · Screen Play by GEORGE WORTHING YATES and RAYMOND T. MARCUS · Screen Story by CURT SIODMAK · Technical Effects by RAY HARRYHAUSEN
Produced by CHARLES H. SCHNEER · Executive Producer: SAM KATZMAN · Directed by FRED F. SEARS · A COLUMBIA PICTURE

THIS SPREAD: (Far Left) US One-sheet (69 x 104cm) Courtesy of Ray Harryhausen Archive. (Above) US Half-sheet (56 x 71cm). (Left) US Window Card (36 x 56cm) Courtesy of Ray Harryhausen Archive.

NEXT SPREAD: PAGE 56 Belgian (36 x 48cm) Courtesy of Mike Hankin Archive. PAGE 57 Swedish (69 x 104cm) Art by V. Lipniunas.

CHAPTER FIVE **EARTH VS THE FLYING SAUCERS**

55

ENFANTS
NON
ADMIS
VARIETES
ENFANTS
NON
ADMIS
25, rue de Malines, Téléph. 17.67.34
Columbia Films S.A.B. présente:
L'INVASION DES
SOUCOUPES VOLANTES
(EARTH vs. THE FLYING SAUCERS)
AVEC
Hugh
Joan
MARLOWE • TAYLOR
et Donald CURTIS
Effets techniques créés par
Ray HARRYHAUSEN
Producteur exécutif
Sam KATZMAN
Mise en scène de
Fred F. SEARS
"LA PALETTE" Brux. Tél. 18.03.87
De INVASIE van de VLIEGENDE SCHOTELS

CHAPTER FIVE **EARTH VS THE FLYING SAUCERS**

58

HARRYHAUSEN THE MOVIE POSTERS

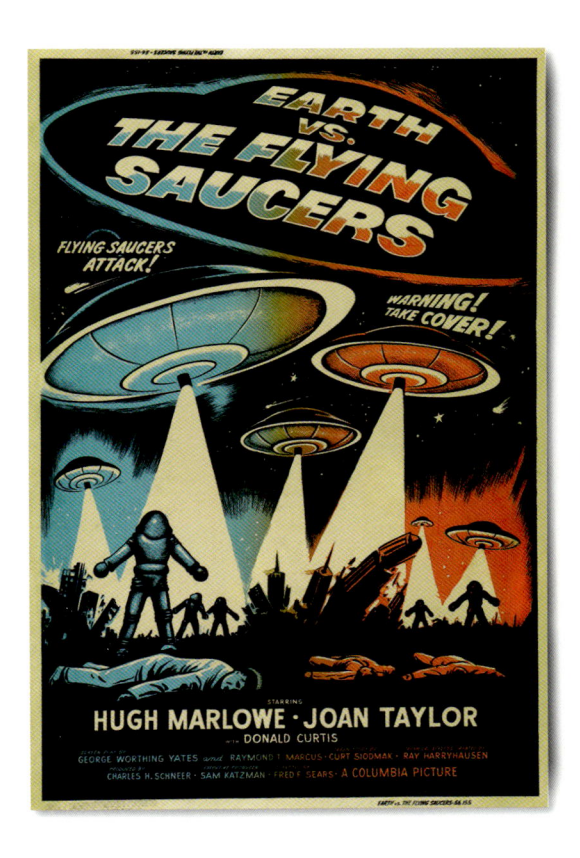

THIS SPREAD: (Opposite) German A1 (58 x 84cm). (Above) British Quad (76 x 102cm) Courtesy of Peter Douglass Archive. (Far Left) US (101 x 152cm). (Left) Italian 2 Fogli (99 x 140cm) Art by Anselmo Ballester.

CHAPTER FIVE **EARTH VS THE FLYING SAUCERS**

20 MILLION MILES TO EARTH

After conducting a most spectacular interplanetary war on a miniscule budget, Ray's third and final black and white science fiction film for Columbia is considered by many of his fans as the most competent of the three. *20 Million Miles to Earth* includes some of the best stop-motion work of Ray's early career, and brings to the screen a creature with tremendous personality.

Culled from various ideas and projects that Ray had been toying with over a number of years, the story tells of an invader from the planet Venus, who is brought back to Earth inside an egg. Breaking free, it grows like the fabled beanstalk into a giant predatory monster. Called an Ymir, the Venusian is a biped with a human torso, a gargoyle-like face, the legs of a satyr and the tail of a dinosaur. Ray brilliantly animates early scenes in which the tiny creature staggers around a tabletop shielding its eyes from the light. Likewise, when the creature has grown to the size of a man, it takes on a more nightmarish appearance. Finally, when transformed into a colossal six-meter high beast, it rampages through Rome before meeting its demise at the hands of the military atop the crumbling façade of the Colosseum. Yet, as it plummets to the ground amid a shower of toppled masonry, the audience feels saddened by its death, in much the same way that Kong's fall from the Empire State Building evoked our sympathies.

THIS PAGE: (Above) One of Ray's pre-production drawings of the Ymir rampaging through Rome. (Below) While less colorful than its American counterparts, the British Quad shows the monster in its entirety. Courtesy of Peter Douglass Archive.

Italy was chosen as the setting for the story, as Ray thought the location more interesting than returning to decimate another American metropolis. The script was by Robert Williams (who had penned numerous scripts for B-western movies) and Christopher Knopf (*The Choirboys*). Nathan Juran (*How Green Was My Valley*) was assigned as the director, and having already helmed a number of low-budget fantasy movies and television series he was well versed in the field of special effects.

Filming took place in Rome during the autumn of 1956, and the cast included William Hopper (*The Deadly Mantis*) as Colonel Robert Calder, the military hero assigned to hunt down the Ymir, and Joan Taylor (*Earth Vs. the Flying Saucers*) as the love interest, Marisa Leonardo. Italian actor Frank Puglia plays the role of the curious scientist Dr. Leonardo.

Once again, Ray's father constructed the steel armature for the Ymir, over which Ray added a pliable foam-rubber body. Although two models were built, one six inches high and the other twelve inches high, it was the latter that was used for the majority of the complex stop-motion scenes, including the heart-pounding moment when the creature confronts the Italian military in the grounds of the Colosseum.

Miniatures of famous Italian buildings were constructed with a similar wire technique to that used in *Earth Vs. the Flying Saucers* to destroy them frame by frame. This process is used to its full advantage when the Ymir crashes through the pillars of the Temple of Saturn, a scene that made the transition from one of Ray's preproduction drawings to finished film almost intact. For the sequence when the Venusian invader battles an escaped elephant on the streets of Rome, Ray built an extremely lifelike stop-motion model. The master animator also designed the spaceship that crashes into the sea, which he based on the available rocket technology of the day.

The first film for Schneer's company, Morningside, *20 Million Miles to Earth* opened through Columbia Pictures in July 1957, on a double-bill with a science fiction movie called *The 27th Day*. But the colorful American artwork concentrated on the lower half of the creature, keeping its facial features a secret. Unlike the film poster art, the tie-in novelization showed the Ymir in full, holding a scantily clad girl in his claw. This image cropped up on the more cartoonish looking Danish poster (*Uhyret Fra Verdensrummet*).

The UK quad poster also showed the creature in its entirety, holding a lamppost in one hand and a man in the other. Anselmo Ballester's striking poster art for the Italian release of the film (*a 30 millioni di Km. Dalla Terra*) dramatically captures the moment when the giant spacecraft returning from the planet Venus plunges into the Mediterranean.

Some of these posters advertise the movie as being filmed in MegaScope. Although it wasn't shot in any of the popular widescreen processes of the day cropped prints were distributed in some European countries (with the exception of his 1964 movie, *First Men in the Moon*, Ray vigorously avoided widescreen due to its incompatibility with his stop-motion process). MegaScope was also the widescreen format used almost exclusively by UK company Hammer Films between 1958 and 1964.

Although trade magazine *Variety* said the film was "Another 'monster' movie to scare the kids the way they like to be scared", *20 Million Miles to Earth* was given an X certificate in Britain and toured the country in December 1957 on the ABC cinema circuit as the supporting feature to the supernatural shocker *Night of the Demon* (a film, incidentally, which Ray had once been approached to work on). Unlike Ray's other 1950s black and white films for Columbia, *20 Million Miles to Earth* was given an American re-release in 1972. It had, of course, already been shown on American television, but UK audiences had to wait until 1969 for its small-screen debut on commercial television (*It Came From Beneath the Sea* followed in 1974 and *Earth Vs. the Flying Saucers* in 1975).

THIS PAGE: (Bottom Left) The American double-bill Campaign Book cover. (Bottom Right) The US One-sheet Style B poster.

CHAPTER FIVE **20 MILLION MILES TO EARTH**   61

OUT-OF-SPACE
CREATURE
INVADES
THE
EARTH!
20 MILLION MILES
TO EARTH
starring
WILLIAM HOPPER • JOAN TAYLOR
Screen Play by BOB WILLIAMS and CHRISTOPHER KNOPF • Story by CHARLOTT KNIGHT
Technical Effects Created by RAY HARRYHAUSEN
Produced by CHARLES H. SCHNEER • Directed by NATHAN JURAN
A MORNINGSIDE PRODUCTION • A COLUMBIA PICTURE

CHAPTER FIVE **20 MILLION MILES TO EARTH**

LA COLUMBIA PICTURES PRESENTA.
BALLESTER
a 30 milioni di Km.
DALLA TERRA
con WILLIAM HOPPER · JOAN TAYLOR
SCENEGGIATURA DI
BOB WILLIAMS e CHRISTOPHER KNOPF
SOGGETTO DI CHARLOTT KNIGHT
EFFETTI TECNICI DI RAY HARRYHAUSEN
MEGASCOPE
PRODOTTO DA CHARLES H. SCHNEER
REGIA DI NATHAN JURAN
UNA PRODUZIONE MORNINGSIDE
TRATTO DAL ROMANZO OMONIMO DI HENRY SLESAR EDITO DA MONDADORI NELLA COLLEZIONE URANIA
COLUMBIA CEIAD

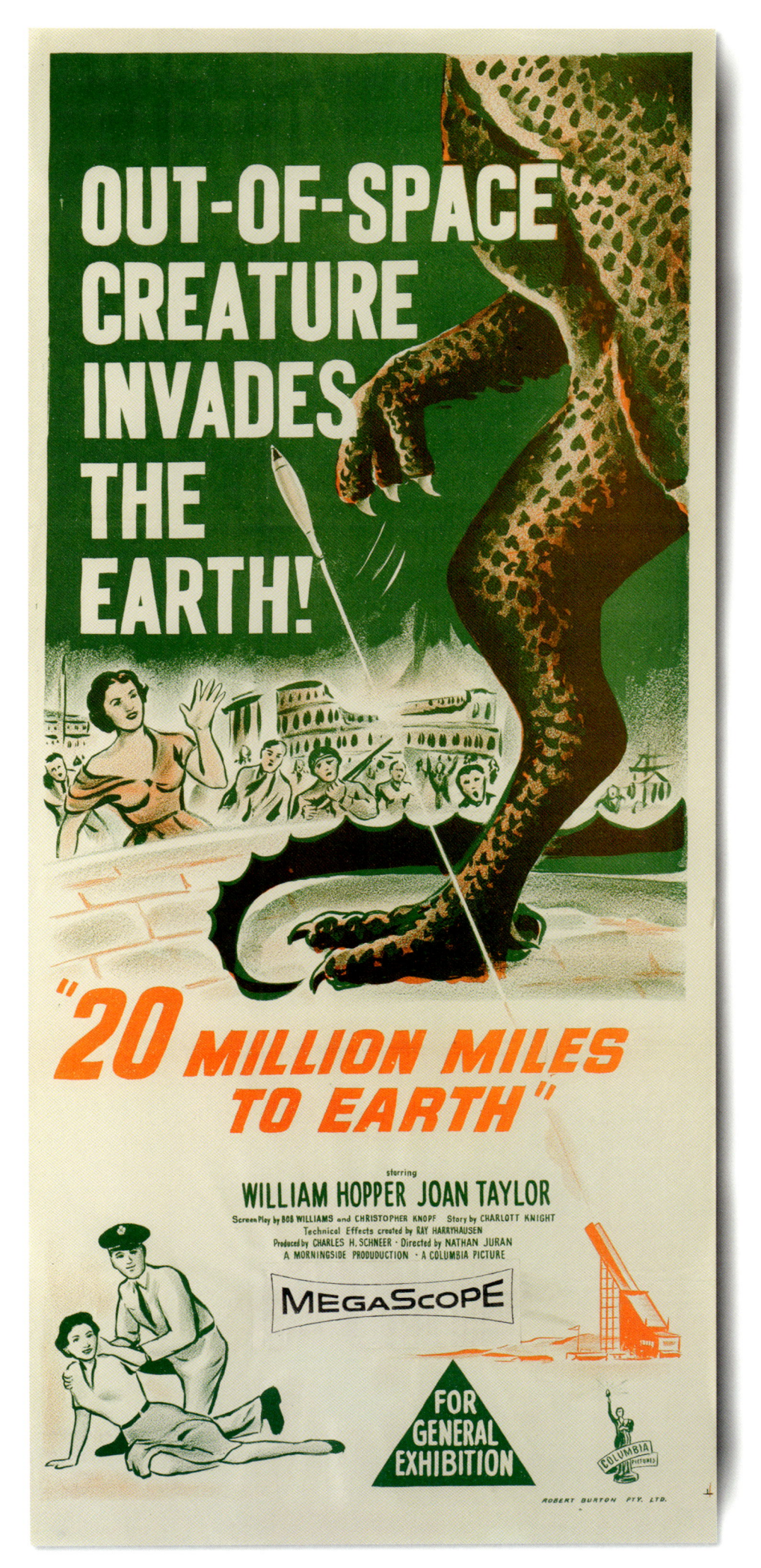

PREVIOUS SPREAD: PAGE 62 US One-sheet (69 x 104cm) Courtesy of Ray Harryhausen Archive. PAGE 63 US (101 x 152cm).

THIS SPREAD: (Far Left) Italian 2 Fogli (99 x 104cm) Art by Anselmo Ballester. (Left) Australian Daybill (34 x 77cm) Courtesy of Ray Harryhausen Archive. (Above) International One-sheet (69 x 104cm) Courtesy of John Ulakovic Archive.

CHAPTER FIVE **20 MILLION MILES TO EARTH** 65

HARRYHAUSEN THE MOVIE POSTERS

THIS SPREAD: (Far Left) German A1 (58 x 84cm) Courtesy of Mike Siegel Archive. (Above) British Quad (76 x 102cm). (Left) Danish (62 x 85cm).

CHAPTER FIVE **20 MILLION MILES TO EARTH**

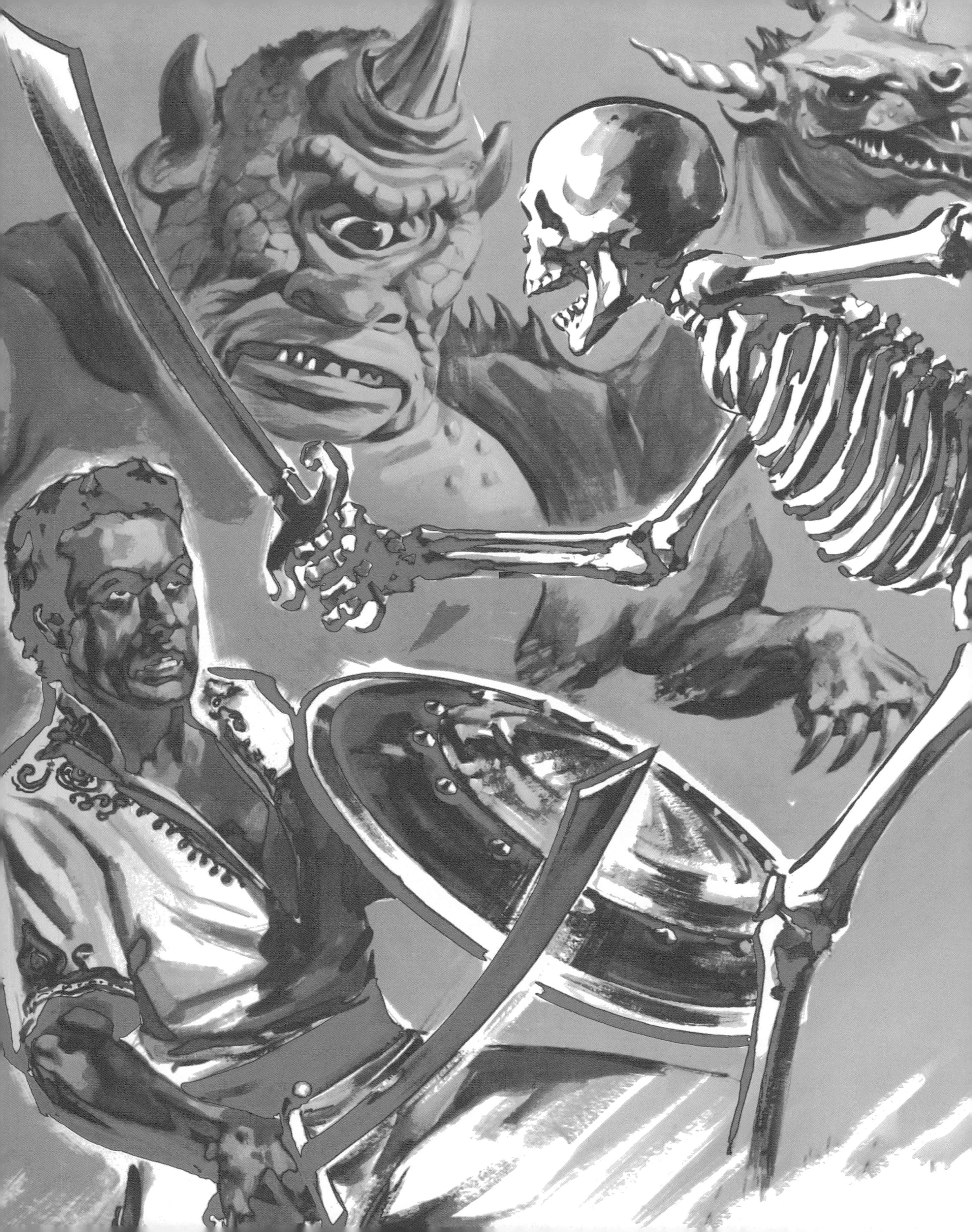

CHAPTER SIX

THE 7ᵀᴴ VOYAGE OF SINBAD (1958)

SPECIAL VISUAL EFFECTS: RAY HARRYHAUSEN

Sinbad the Sailor sets sail for Persia with his fiancée Princess Parisa. Stopping off on the Isle of Colossa for fresh supplies, the crew is attacked by a giant cyclops. Rescued by Sokurah, a magician who summons a Genie from a magic lamp to stop the monster, they manage to escape. But having lost the lamp in the scuffle, Sokurah casts a magic spell that reduces Parisa to the size of a mouse, insisting that Sinbad must return to Colossa for the antidote. But Sinbad must face all manner of dangers in order to rescue the princess, including the cyclops, a giant two-headed bird called a Roc, a sword-fighting skeleton and the guardian of Sokurah's castle, a monstrous fire-breathing dragon.

8TH WONDER OF THE SCREEN!

Ray had always admired the work of French illustrator Gustave Doré (1832–1883). One of Dore's drawings showed a knight atop a spiral staircase, from which Ray dreamt up the idea of the man fighting a skeleton warrior. He even thought that it would make a perfect stop-motion scene in a film based on the *Arabian Nights* stories, in particular the mythical voyages of Sinbad the Sailor.

When Charles Schneer inquired about new story ideas to capitalise on the success of *20 Million Miles to Earth*, Ray showed him the outline and preliminary drawings that he'd prepared for the Sinbad project. Schneer was so enthused with the concept that he immediately hired television scriptwriter Kenneth Kolb to write a screenplay.

Kolb met with Ray and together the two fleshed out a storyline to include an evil sorcerer, a princess, a giant Roc (two-headed bird), a Cyclops, a dragon and a sword-wielding skeleton. With the script finalised in June 1957, Ray was ready to start work on the stop-motion, but needed some persuading when Schneer opined that the film should be made in Technicolor. Ray was uncertain whether his type of special effects — the magical combination of film elements that successfully integrated his stop-motion creatures with live action — would work in color, so he spent several weeks testing the process. Fortunately the results were perfect, and Columbia Pictures gave the green light and a budget of six hundred thousand dollars so work could begin on Ray's sixth feature film, *The 7th Voyage of Sinbad*.

THIS PAGE: (Above) Marquee advertizing the film in New York. (Below) US lobby card showing the fight between Sinbad and the skeleton, a scene cut from the UK release.

HARRYHAUSEN THE MOVIE POSTERS

The studio suggested contract player Kerwin Mathews (*Jack the Giant Killer*) to play Sinbad, which was fortuitous for Ray as the young actor showed tremendous skill in shadowboxing the imaginary fight scenes. In other words, Mathews was extremely skilled in reacting to creatures that wouldn't be added until post-production. His understanding of what was required for the stop-motion scenes was particularly apparent during the sword fight between Sinbad and a human skeleton. The interplay between the actor and the stop-motion figure in the finished film is flawless, thanks to the duel being meticulously choreographed in advance.

Kathryn Grant (*Anatomy of a Murder*) was cast as Sinbad's love interest, Princess Parisa, while veteran character actor Torin Thatcher (*Jack the Giant Killer*) played the evil magician, Sokurah. Child star Richard Eyre (*The Invisible Boy*) was also brought in to play the benevolent Genie. The production team included Nathan Juran (*20 Million Miles to Earth*) as the director, Wilkie Cooper (*Stage Fright*) as the cinematographer and Bernard Herrmann (*Psycho*) as the composer.

The live-action elements of the film were shot in Spain, with locations on the Costa Brava and the island of Mallorca. The then unspoiled beauty of the Mediterranean coastline and its mountainous terrain proved to be ideal settings for the mythical lands featured in the story.

After the filming in Spain was completed, the blue-screen elements necessary to help Ray combine his stop-motion figures with the previously shot live-action scenes were carried out at the MGM studios in England. Ray then returned to his customized studio in Los Angeles, where he spent the next eight months working on the special effects. Ray's father constructed the metal armatures for each of the creatures, with Ray and his assistant George Lofgren (*The Beast From 20,000 Fathoms*) using a foam-injection molding technique to sculpt the final models.

The creatures that Ray constructed for the film included a horned Cyclops with cloven hooves and three-fingered claws, a dancing snake woman called Sadi, a Giant Roc and its equally monstrous offspring (which snatches up Sinbad in its massive talons), and a fire-breathing dragon (that bears more than a passing resemblance to Ray's Rhedosaurus in *The Beast From 20,000 Fathoms*). In the film's stunning climax, a ferocious battle takes place between the dragon and the Cyclops, which took Ray almost three weeks to animate.

The highlight of the movie, however, and another example of Ray's skill with stop-motion animation, is the sequence where Sokurah conjures up a living skeleton to challenge Sinbad. The result of the confrontation between hero and villain is a sword fight that reaches its breathtaking climax in a scene set at the top of a spiral staircase, inspired so many years earlier by Doré's art. To achieve the effect, Mathews rehearsed the fight with Olympic fencing champion Enzo Musumeci Greco, before the actor was filmed fighting solo. This footage was then combined with Ray's nine-inch-high model skeleton via rear projection and split-screen; a task that took almost three months to complete. The result, accompanied by composer Hermann's unique musical score (referred to as the 'castanet concerto') is a visual *tour de force*.

One important addition to the film's publicity was the introduction of the word 'Dynamation' to describe Ray's proprietary special effects process. With the industry full of grandiose titles such as Cinemascope, Cinerama, Technirama 70, and Panavision, Schneer had dreamt up the name by combining the words 'Dyna', from the name Dynaflow on the dashboard of his Buick motor car, and 'animation'. Dynamation certainly caused a buzz with the critics and would subsequently be used in the advertising for all of Ray's movies, except *One Million Years B.C.* and *Clash of the Titans,* or when it was retitled as either Superdynamation or Dynarama.

The 7th Voyage of Sinbad opened in America for Christmas 1958 to rave reviews, and went on to make six million dollars worldwide. It toured on a general release with another Columbia film, a wartime drama called *Ghost of the China Sea*. It opened in Britain at the Metropole Victoria in London and was subsequently released through the Gaumont cinema circuit on a double-bill with a western entitled *The Hard Man*. In order to secure a U certificate, the British Board of Film Censors cut the entire skeleton sequence, along with some of the Cyclops footage. When the film was re-released in May 1963, on a double-bill with *The 3 Worlds of Gulliver*, the skeleton scene was still missing.

When Ray, Schneer and Columbia returned to the Sinbad saga in the 1970s with *The Golden Voyage of Sinbad*, *The 7th Voyage of Sinbad* was re-released uncut and with new poster art. In America it was released on a double-bill with the fantasy drama *Chosen Survivors*, while in the UK (having already made its commercial television debut in 1971) it accompanied the comedy *Watch Out, We're Mad* for a successful run on the Odeon cinema circuit.

The American poster art for the original release in 1958 captured the thrill-packed elements of the film, with a large image of the leading actors backed by some exciting scenes from the movie. Once again it was the European artwork that differed from the norm. In Italy, the posters (*Il 7 Viaggio Di Sinbad*) featured prominent images of the Giant Roc, the dragon, the Cyclops and the skeleton. Likewise, the German poster (*Sindbads 7. Reise*) also made the skeleton fight a key selling point in the film's promotion. The East German poster (*Sinbads Siebente Reise)* with art by Vonderwerth captures the classic style of the *Arabian Nights* stories with a turbaned Sinbad in the mouth of the dragon.

The British quad poster is a stylish piece of artwork by an unknown artist, but must have confused audiences as it does include the skeleton fight. While the majority of American and European posters used the same artwork for the mid-1970s re-release, the Japanese poster, although resorting to photographic images, offers an almost full-figure shot of the Cyclops.

For the film's 1975 re-release, British artist Brian Bysouth painted a very atmospheric poster of Sinbad and Parisa at the ship's wheel. This artwork subsequently appeared on a number of international posters, including the French version (*Le 7e Voyage de Sinbad*). Although all the 1958 publicity had highlighted the Dynamation process, describing it as the 'Newest Movie-Making Miracle', the name was changed to Dynarama for the 1970s re-release posters.

THIS PAGE: (Above) Sinbad is carried aloft by the two-headed Roc. Ray constructed a tiny stop-motion figure of Sinbad for these special effects scenes.

CHAPTER SIX **THE 7TH VOYAGE OF SINBAD**

ADVENTURE OF THE AGES – FOR ALL AGES
IN
DYNAMATION!
THE 7th VOYAGE OF SINBAD
TECHNICOLOR®
starring
KERWIN MATHEWS · KATHRYN GRANT
co-starring RICHARD EYER, AS THE GENIE with TORIN THATCHER
Written by KENNETH KOLB · Visual Effects Created by RAY HARRYHAUSEN · Produced by CHARLES H. SCHNEER · Directed by NATHAN JURAN
A MORNINGSIDE PRODUCTION · A COLUMBIA PICTURE

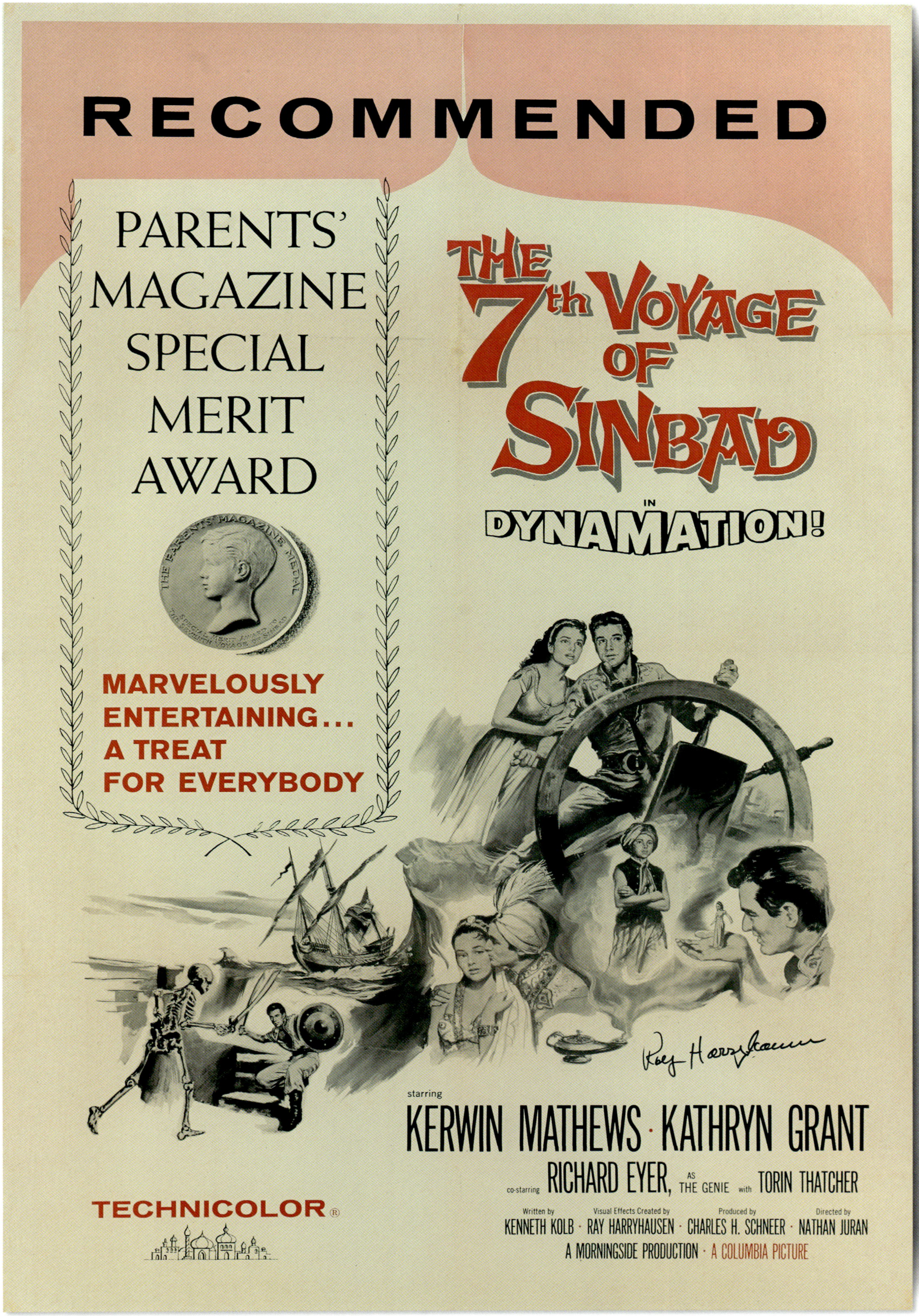

HARRYHAUSEN THE MOVIE POSTERS

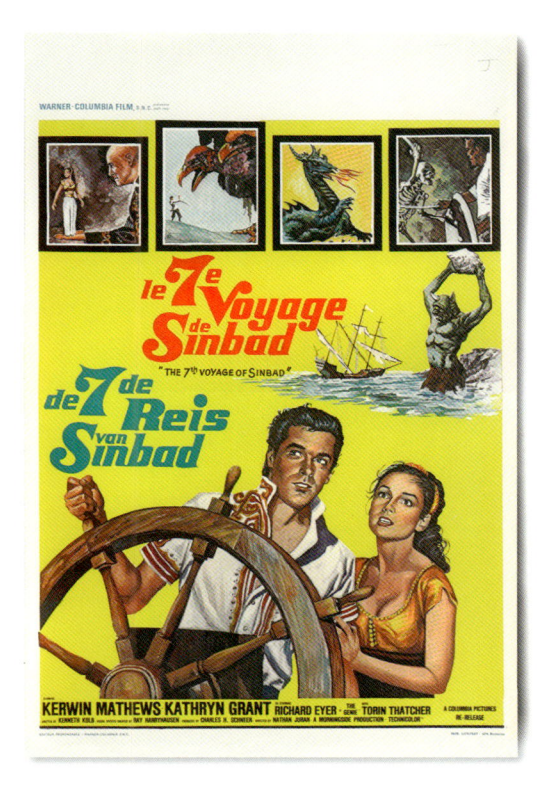

PREVIOUS SPREAD: PAGE 72 US One-sheet (69 x 104cm) Courtesy of Andy Johnson Archive. PAGE 73 US One-sheet (69 x 104cm) Courtesy of Andy Johnson Archive.

THIS SPREAD: (Opposite Above) British Quad (76 x 102cm) Courtesy of Mark Mawston Archive. (Opposite Below) Belgian (36 x 48cm) Courtesy of Mike Hankin Archive. (Left) Locandina (35 x 68cm) Courtesy of Neil Pettigrew Archive. (Top Right) Spanish (70 x 99cm) Courtesy of eMoviePoster.com/Hershenson/Allen Archive. (Bottom Right) Belgian (36 x 48cm) Courtesy of Mike Hankin Archive.

CHAPTER SIX **THE 7TH VOYAGE OF SINBAD**

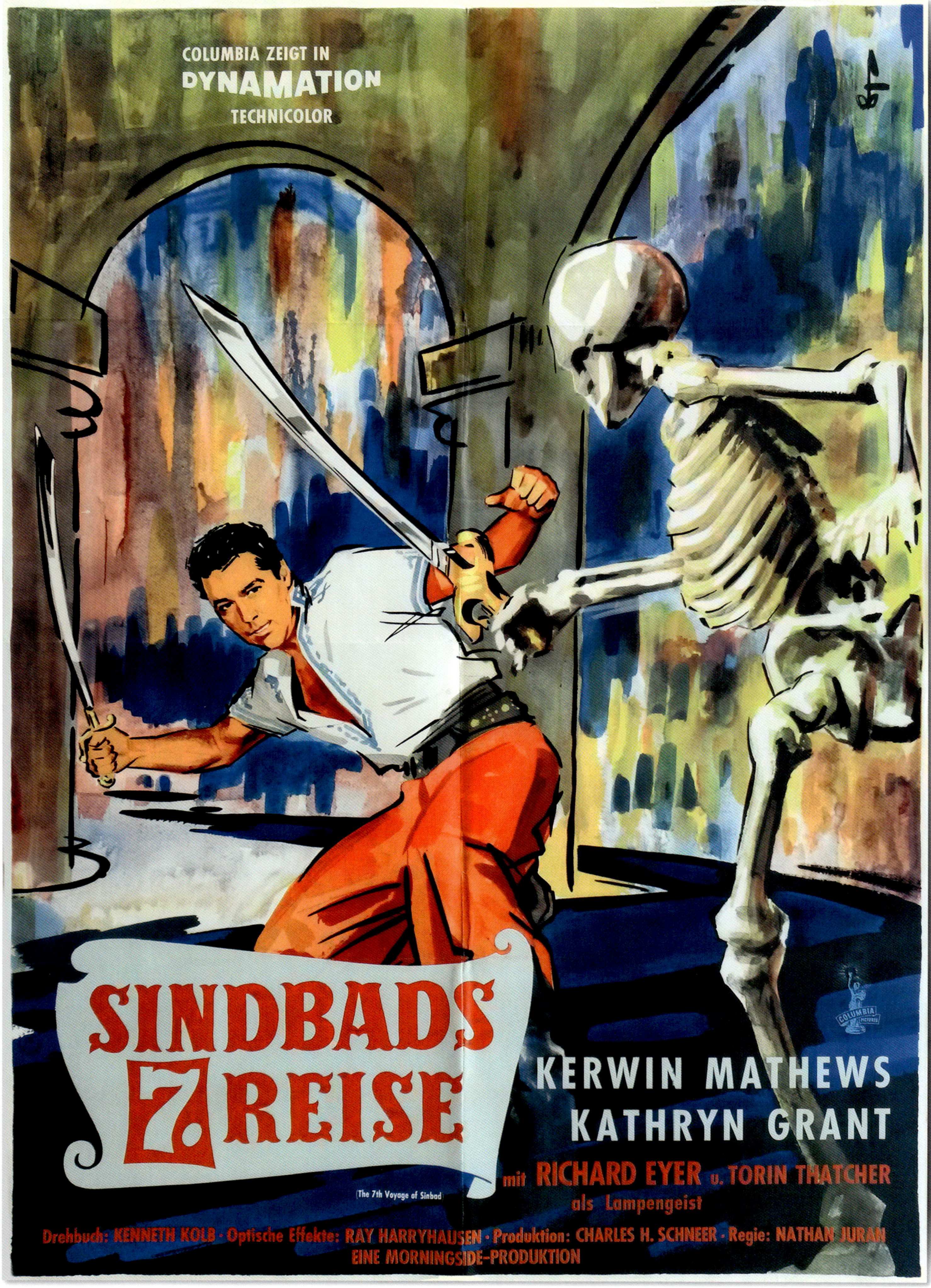
COLUMBIA ZEIGT IN
DYNAMATION
TECHNICOLOR
SINDBADS 7. REISE
(The 7th Voyage of Sinbad)
KERWIN MATHEWS
KATHRYN GRANT
mit RICHARD EYER u. TORIN THATCHER
als Lampengeist
Drehbuch: KENNETH KOLB · Optische Effekte: RAY HARRYHAUSEN · Produktion: CHARLES H. SCHNEER · Regie: NATHAN JURAN
EINE MORNINGSIDE-PRODUKTION

CHAPTER SIX **THE 7TH VOYAGE OF SINBAD**

HARRYHAUSEN THE MOVIE POSTERS

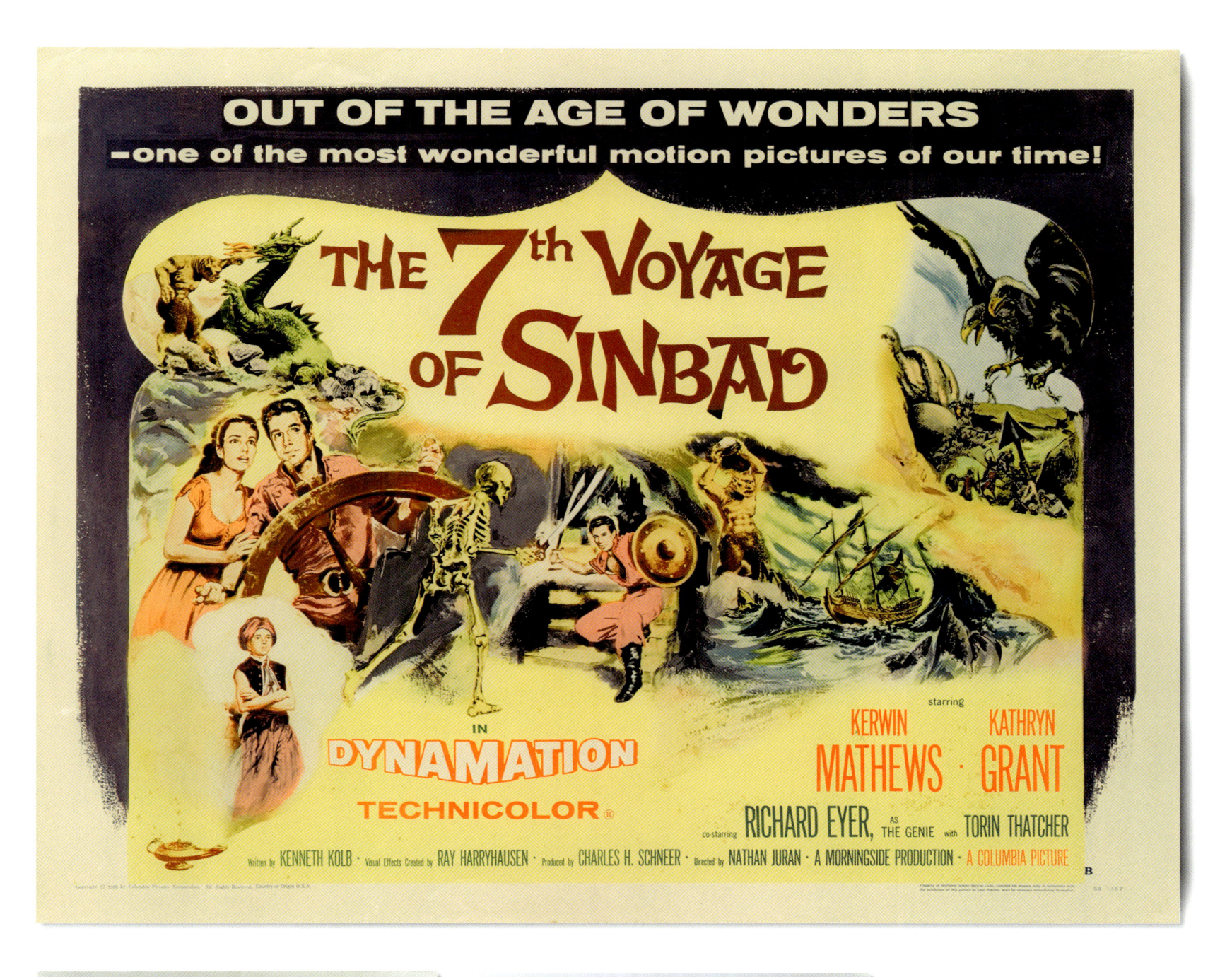

PREVIOUS SPREAD: PAGE 76 German A1 (58 x 84cm) Courtesy of Mike Siegel Archive. PAGE 77 Italian 2 Fogli (99 x 140cm).

THIS SPREAD: (Opposite) East German (58 x 84cm) Courtesy of Jens Holzheuer Archive. (Above) US Half-sheet Style B (56 x 71cm) Courtesy of Ray Harryhausen Archive. (Bottom Left) French Grande (115 x 157cm) Courtesy of Ray Harryhausen Archive. (Bottom Right) Pakistan (69 x 104cm) Courtesy of John Ulakovic Archive.

NEXT SPREAD: PAGE 80 Italian 2 Fogli (99 x 140cm) PAGE 81 Japanese B2 (51 x 76cm) Courtesy of Ray Harryhausen Archive.

CHAPTER SIX **THE 7TH VOYAGE OF SINBAD**

LA COLUMBIA PICTURES PRESENTA
UNA SPETTACOLARE AVVENTURA REALIZZATA NELLA MAGIA DEL
DYNAMATION
IL 7° VIAGGIO DI SINBAD
IN DYNAMATION
CON
KERWIN MATHEWS
KATHRYN GRANT
E CON RICHARD EYER, NEL RUOLO DEL "GENIO" CON TORIN THATCHER
SCRITTO DA KENNETH KOLB • EFFETTI SPECIALI CREATI DA RAY HARRYHAUSEN • PRODOTTO DA CHARLES H. SCHNEER • DIRETTO DA NATHAN JURAN
UNA PRODUZIONE MORNINGSIDE • TECHNICOLOR®
CEIAD COLUMBIA
PRIMA EDIZIONE ITALIANA 1976

CHAPTER SIX **THE 7TH VOYAGE OF SINBAD**

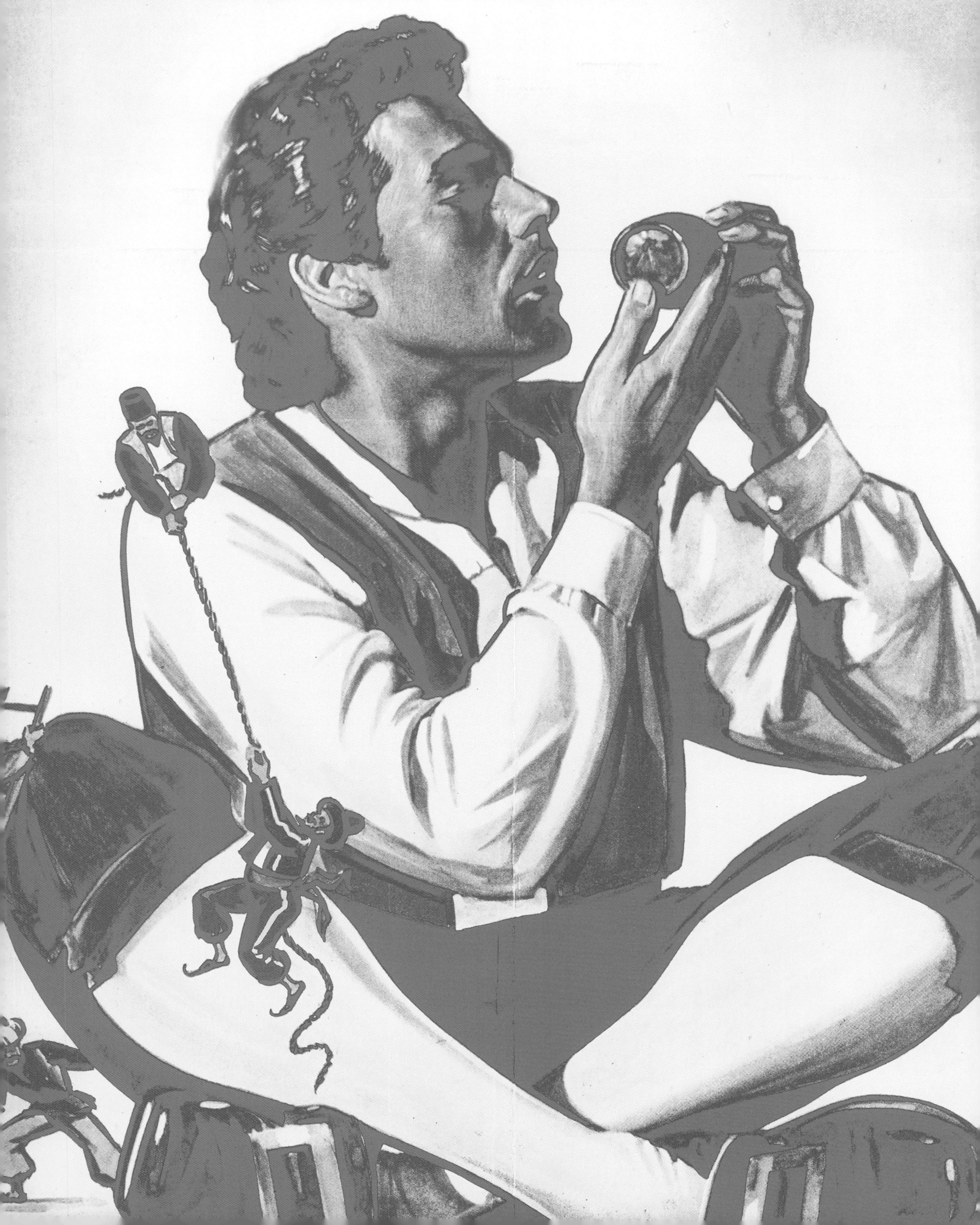

CHAPTER SEVEN

THE 3 WORLDS OF GULLIVER (1960) MYSTERIOUS ISLAND (1961)

SPECIAL VISUAL EFFECTS: RAY HARRYHAUSEN

THE 3 WORLDS OF GULLIVER: In dire financial straits and against the wishes of his fiancée Elizabeth, Dr. Lemuel Gulliver signs up to be a ship's surgeon, but is swept overboard during a storm. Washed up on an unknown island, he finds himself the prisoner of a tiny race of people called Lilliputians. He finally manages to win their friendship by averting a war between Lilliput and its neighbor Blefuscu when he tows the enemy ships out to sea. Leaving the strange land, Gulliver is then marooned on another island populated by giants called Brobdingnagians, who accuse their miniscule visitor of witchcraft and force him into a life-or-death struggle with the King's pet crocodile. Finally reunited with Elizabeth, Gulliver begins to wonder if his fantastic adventures were only a dream.

MYSTERIOUS ISLAND: During the American Civil War, a news correspondent, a Confederate guard and a group of Union soldiers escape captivity in an observation balloon. After being caught in a storm they're washed ashore on an uncharted volcanic island. Rescuing two women from a shipwreck, the survivors build an elaborate campsite from where they fight off a band of marauding pirates. Unfortunately the island is also home to some giant creatures, including a crab, a prehistoric bird called a Phorohacos, giant bees, and a multi-tentacled sea beast. All of which are the result of experiments by another castaway, the infamous Captain Nemo. When a volcanic eruption threatens to sink the island, they enlist the captain's help in order to escape.

A MIRACLE IN MOTION PICTURES!
THE 3 WORLDS OF GULLIVER

Fresh from the box office success of *The 7th Voyage of Sinbad*, Ray began work on a series of drawings for a new script about the hero of Jonathan Swift's 18th-century novel *Gulliver's Travels*. Schneer had already purchased the rights from Universal and felt that it was a perfect subject for Ray's Dynamation process.

Kerwin Mathews (*The 7th Voyage of Sinbad*) returned to play the lead role, with a supporting cast that included June Thorburn (*Tom Thumb*) as Elizabeth Whitley, and popular leading man Lee Patterson (*Reach for the Sky*) as Reldresal. Composer Bernard Herrmann was again assigned to write the score, which added greatly to the overall impact of the finished film.

The 3 Worlds of Gulliver also marked a new era for Ray, when he and Schneer moved their film operation from Los Angeles to London. The key reason for the decision was the close proximity of the European locations, used to such great effect in *The 7th Voyage of Sinbad*. Another deciding factor was the definite advantages the Rank Film Laboratories' sodium vapor system could offer Ray's Dynamation process. Licensed to Disney for films such as *The Absent-Minded Professor* and *Mary Poppins*, the sodium backing traveling matte process, as it was also known, was so successful that Ray used it again on his next two films: *Mysterious Island* and *Jason and the Argonauts*.

THIS PAGE: (Above) Gulliver finds himself at the mercy of the giants in the magical land of Brobdingnag. (Below) The film was also the subject of a tie-in comic book published by Dell.

Under the direction of Jack Sher (*The Wild and the Innocent*), the production crew moved to Spain, shooting live-action sequences on S'Agaro beach, at a chateau in Segovia, in the walled city of Avilla and in the mountains of Boca del Asno. Additional miniature work was also shot in Madrid's Sevilla Film Studios. The remaining live action, including interiors, was filmed at Pinewood Studios, with Ray making the latter his home to complete the stop-motion effects.

With Gulliver changing size depending on which magical land he finds himself in, the film required some 300 traveling mattes. However, Ray would occasionally resort to tried and trusted in-camera methods such as forced perspective. This simple technique could create the illusion of a giant figure among miniature people without the need for any complicated optical work.

Unlike *The 7th Voyage of Sinbad*, the film only features two stop-motion creatures. When Gulliver finds himself trapped as a tiny figure in Brobdingnag, he encounters an inquisitive squirrel and then has to fight off a very unfriendly alligator armed with nothing more than a jewellery box latch pin as a sword and a brooch as a shield.

The 3 Worlds of Gulliver was given a Royal Premiere in London, at the Odeon, Marble Arch in November 1960. It then opened across the UK (with Western adventure *Seven Ways From Sundown*) on the Odeon circuit, and an American nationwide release in time for Christmas. Poster art for the film varied widely from country to country, with some impressive designs by artist Deseta for the Italian release (*I Viaggi di Gulliver*).

The UK quad poster showed Gulliver among the tiny inhabitants of Lilliput, while the American one-sheet poster opted instead for scenes from the film, behind which Gulliver's legs can be seen striding the Earth. Columbia also spent a great deal of time and effort in regard to merchandising, with book tie-ins, apparel and novelties, as well as extensive television advertising and a float in Macy's Thanksgiving Day Parade in New York. *The 3 Worlds of Gulliver* was re-released in 1963 as the supporting programme to *The 7th Voyage of Sinbad*, but it would be another decade before it made its UK commercial television debut in 1974.

CHAPTER SEVEN **THE 3 WORLDS OF GULLIVER**

HARRYHAUSEN THE MOVIE POSTERS

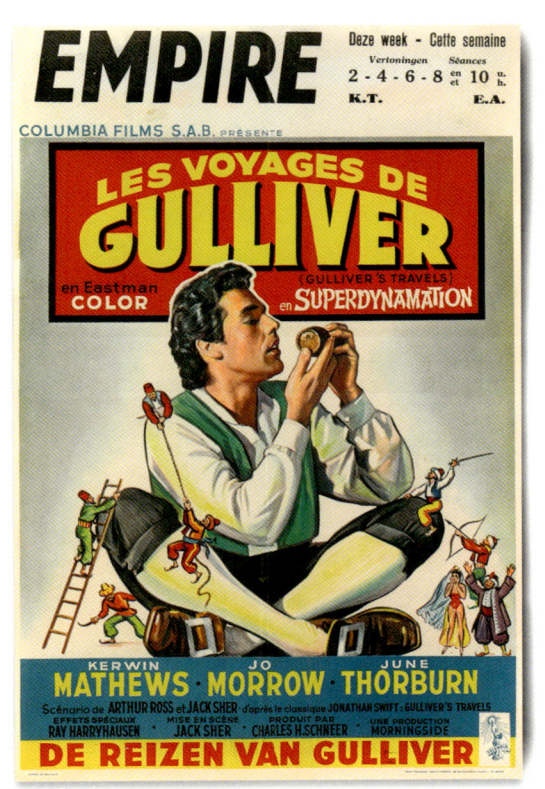

PREVIOUS PAGE: PAGE 85 US One-sheet (69 x 104cm)
Courtesy of Simon Greetham Archive.

THIS SPREAD: (Opposite) Australian One-sheet (69 x 104cm).
(Above) US Half-sheet Style B (56 x 71cm) Courtesy of Paul White Archive.
(Left) Belgian (36 x 48cm) Courtesy of Mike Hankin Archive.

CHAPTER SEVEN **THE 3 WORLDS OF GULLIVER**

HARRYHAUSEN THE MOVIE POSTERS

CHAPTER SEVEN **THE 3 WORLDS OF GULLIVER**

NOTHING LESS THAN A MIRACLE
IN MOTION PICTURES!
COLUMBIA PICTURES PRESENTS
THE 3 WORLDS OF
GULLIVER
in
SUPERDYNAMATION
"U"
and TECHNICOLOR®
starring
KERWIN
MATHEWS
JUNE THORBURN · JO MORROW
Visual Effects by
RAY HARRYHAUSEN ·

PREVIOUS SPREAD: PAGE 88 (Clockwise from top left) French Grande (115 x 157cm) Courtesy of Neil Pettigrew Archive. German A1 (58 x 84cm) Art by Hans Drain. Courtesy of Ray Harryhausen Archive. Italian 2 Foglio (99 x 140cm) Art by Enrico De Seta. German A1 (58 x 84cm) Art by Kumpf. Courtesy of Mike Siegel Archive. PAGE 89 Italian Grande (99 x 140cm) Art by Enrico De Seta.

THIS PAGE: (Left) British Quad (76 x 102cm) Courtesy of Simon Greetham Archive. (Above) US Silk-screen (101 x 152cm).

CHAPTER SEVEN **THE 3 WORLDS OF GULLIVER** 91

MYSTERIOUS ISLAND

The novel *The Mysterious Island (L'île mystérieuse)* by 19th-century French author Jules Verne is a sequel of sorts to his highly successful story *20,000 Leagues Under the Sea* and was published in 1874. An abandoned script version of the book came to producer Charles Schneer's attention shortly after the release of *The 7th Voyage of Sinbad*. Showing it to Ray, he decided that it was a suitable project for his newly formed production company Ameran Films Ltd. In the months that followed, the script was rewritten to incorporate a number of stop-motion creatures that Ray wanted to add to the story.

Although he originally planned to make the animal inhabitants of *Mysterious Island* prehistoric in origin, he decided instead on giant animals such as a crab and a bee. Two primordial beasts were included, however, as Ray had already constructed the models; a prehistoric bird called a Phororhacos and an undersea squid-like creature called a Nautiloid Cephalopod. Sculptor Arthur Hayward of London's Museum of Natural History was assigned to make maquettes of the creatures, after which Ray would cast latex bodies to fit over the metal ball-and-socket armatures.

The film is set during the American Civil War and was directed by Cy Endfield (*Zulu*) and photographed by Wilkie Cooper. It stars American actors Gary Merrill (*All About Eve*) as war correspondent Gideon Spilet, and Michael Callan (*Cat Ballou*) as Herbert Brown, a Union soldier and love interest for another of the island's castaways, Elena Puckle, played by newcomer Beth Rogan. Rogan spent much of the film in the skimpiest

THIS PAGE: (Above) Producer Charles Schneer (right with glasses) views the advertising campaign generated by Columbia and Associated British Cinemas (ABC) for *Mysterious Island*. (Below) The castaways encounter a giant crab.

HARRYHAUSEN THE MOVIE POSTERS

of costumes, which was certainly exploited by the studio's campaign book.

British actors in the film included Michael Craig (*The Fast Lady*) in the lead role as granite-jawed Captain Cyrus Harding; husky voiced Joan Greenwood (*Kind Hearts and Coronets*) as Puckle's aristocratic aunt, Lady Mary Fairchild; Percy Herbert (*The Bridge on the River Kwai*) as shanghaied Confederate army sergeant Pencroft; and Dan Jackson (*Flame in the Streets*) as Corporal Neb. Veteran actor Herbert Lom (*Mark of the Devil*) was cast as Captain Nemo, last heard of aboard the doomed submarine *Nautilus*, and the scientist whose experiments with growth serums have resulted in the island's population of giant animals.

As usual, Ray involved himself in all aspects of the production, visiting the beach locations in Spain and advising the actors on what would happen in the scenes featuring his stop-motion creatures. He also spent time devising the escape in the observation balloon at the beginning of the film. This sequence featured a combination of intricate model work, travelling mattes and the actors suspended in a rickety basket in front of the sodium vapor backing system.

The jagged and atmospheric landscape of the island was enhanced by the use of matte paintings (landscapes painted on glass and either placed in front of the camera during shooting or added later by split screen). Under Ray's supervision, these mattes were created by the special effects team at Les Bowie's studio in Slough, along with a miniature of an erupting volcano. Miniatures were also used to represent Nemo's crippled submarine *Nautilus* and an invading pirate ship.

As with all of Ray's previous movies, *Mysterious Island* features many examples of the animator's skill in combining live actors with stop-motion models. The beach sequence for instance, in which a crustacean the size of a truck bursts through the sand, is both dramatic and convincing. Throwing the hapless humans off its back, it turns to face them, jabbing the air with its deadly pincers. The fight that ensues is brought even more to life by composer Bernard Herrmann's music. Similarly, the interaction between the castaways and the giant Phorohacos, when Michael Callan leaps on its back to save Beth Rogan, is a prime example of the perfection Ray had achieved with his Dynamation process.

The film opened in America at the end of 1961, although its release was held back until summer 1962 in the UK. Deciding not to preview the film for the critics, Columbia opened *Mysterious Island* on a double-bill with Hammer's swashbuckling adventure, *The Pirates of Blood River* at the London Pavilion from July 13th. During its West End run, the film was promoted as the A picture, but when the ABC cinema circuit picked up the duo for general release from August 12th it was relegated to second billing (with fewer screenings a day than *Pirates*). However, this was probably more to do with the tremendous box-office success that ABC had enjoyed with previous Hammer releases.

National Screen Services produced two distinctive quad posters. The full quad featured the island, the descending balloon and a nubile Beth Rogan sitting at the feet of Herbert Lom. Closer inspection reveals the title of the film emblazoned across the sky. The double-bill poster is even more striking with bolder colors.

The poster artwork for the film was subtly changed in countries across Europe, but the main image of the descending balloon was included in most. One notable exception, however, is Alfredo Capitani's Italian poster (*L'Isola Misteriosa*). In his version the balloon is skating a stormy sea with the volcanic island in the background. In keeping with mainland Europe's more liberal approach to the feminine angle, Capitani includes Beth Rogan's face looming out of the clouds, although an alternative Italian design, by the same artist, featured the castaways defending themselves against the invading pirate ship.

A late seventies German re-issue poster (*Die geheimnisvolle Insel*) even went so far as to feature prehistoric creatures (including a pterodactyl, and a styracosaurus) and what appears to be a science fiction character resembling Luke Skywalker! A Spanish reissue (*La Isla Misteriosa*), on the other hand, shows the balloon descending on to the head of a giant sea serpent. The French poster by artist Jean Mascii (1926-2003) is particularly striking, as it shows an outline of the island and an underwater creature attacking the castaways. Well known to European audiences, actor Herbert Lom dominates the Belgian poster design (*L'île Mystérieuse*).

Mysterious Island debuted on American television as early as 1965 and in the UK on some regional commercial stations in 1971. Eight years later it was reissued in Britain on a double-bill with the low-budget science fiction film *The Humanoid*, even though Columbia and National Screen Services produced a stunning double-bill poster showing it as the supporting programme to a re-release of *Jason and the Argonauts*.

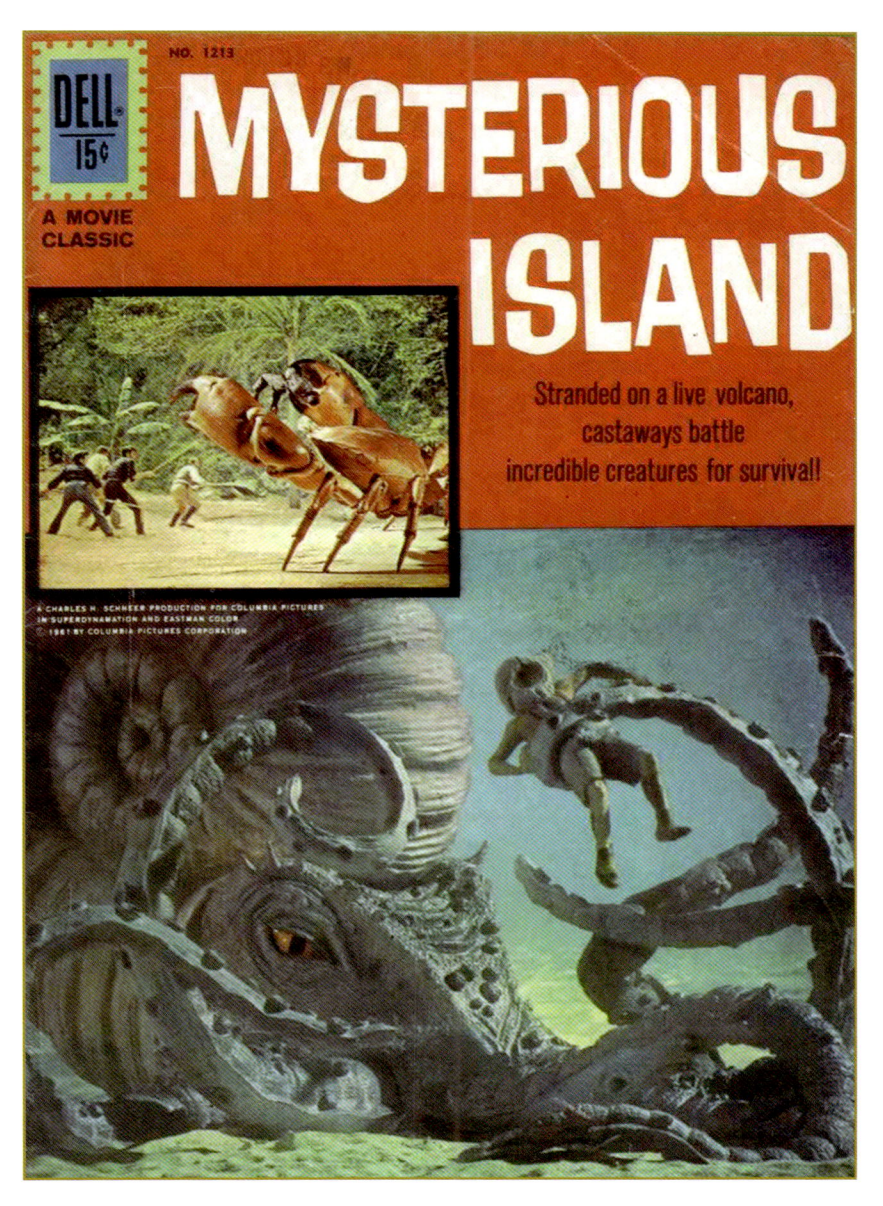

THIS PAGE: (Right) The tie-in Dell comic book featured the film adaptation of the Jules Verne novel.

CHAPTER SEVEN **MYSTERIOUS ISLAND**

94 | HARRYHAUSEN THE MOVIE POSTERS

THIS SPREAD: (Left) US One-sheet (69 x 104cm) Courtesy of Simon Greetham Archive. (Above) US silk-screen (101 x 152cm).

CHAPTER SEVEN **MYSTERIOUS ISLAND**

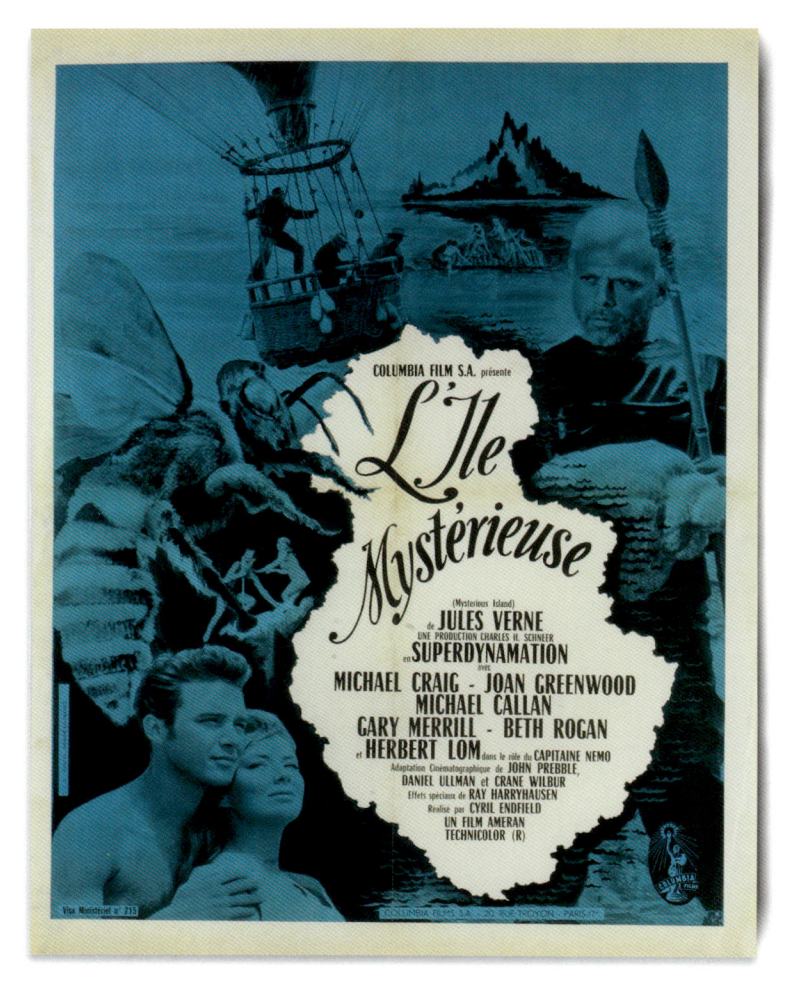

HARRYHAUSEN THE MOVIE POSTERS

LA COLUMBIA PICTURES presenta
COLUMBIA
C.E.I.A.D.
L'ISOLA MISTERIOSA
DI GIULIO VERNE
UNA PRODUZIONE CHARLES H. SCHNEER IN SUPERDYNAMATION
CON MICHAEL CRAIG JOAN GREENWOOD MICHAEL CALLAN GARY MERRILL BETH ROGAN E HERBERT LOM NEL RUOLO DEL CAPITANO NEMO
SCENEGGIATURA DI JOHN PREBBLE, DANIEL ULLMAN E CRANE WILBUR · EFFETTI OTTICI CREATI DA RAY HARRYHAUSEN · REGIA DI CY ENDFIELD · UN FILM AMERAN
EASTMANCOLOR

Wherever YOU are you're
DARING SWASHBUCKLING ADVENTURE!
The Pirates of Blood River
·U·
KERWIN
CHRISTOPHER
GLENN
MATHEWS·LEE·CORBETT
HAMMERSCOPE · TECHNICOLOR
co-starring
PETER ARNE
MARLA LANDI
ANDREW KEIR
OLIVER REED
A Hammer Film Production A Columbia Picture
A BLC RELEASE
a Charles
starring Michae
Gary Merrill
THE GREATEST
ALL
COLOUR!
ACTION!
ADVENTURE!
GIANT
Printed in England

PREVIOUS SPREAD: PAGE 96 (Clockwise from top left) Belgian (36 x 48cm) Courtesy of Mike Hankin Archive. French Grande (115 x 157cm) Art by Boris Grinsson. French Affiche Moyenne (60 x 80cm) Courtesy of Ray Harryhausen Archive. German A1 (58 x 84cm) Courtesy of Neil Pettigrew Archive. PAGE 97 Italian 2 Fogli (99 x 140cm) Art by Alfredo Capitani.

THIS SPREAD: (Left) British Quad (76 x 102cm) Courtesy of Simon Greetham Archive. (Above) German A1 (58 x 84cm) Art by G. Meerwald. Courtesy of Neil Pettigrew Archive.

NEXT SPREAD: PAGE 100 Spanish (70 x 99cm) Courtesy of Neil Pettigrew Archive. PAGE 101 US One-sheet (69x104cm) Courtesy of Ray Harryhausen Archive.

CHAPTER SEVEN **MYSTERIOUS ISLAND**

99

COLUMBIA PICTURES presenta
La Isla Misteriosa
(MYSTERIOUS ISLAND)
¡LA FANTASIA DE UN GENIO SOÑADOR CONVERTIDA EN REALIDAD!
¡AVENTURAS QUE DESAFIAN A LA IMAGINACION!
Basada en la famosa novela de
JULIO VERNE
Una Producción de CHARLES H. SCHNEER
MICHAEL CRAIG • JOAN GREENWOOD • MICHAEL CALLAN • GARY MERRILL
BETH ROGAN y HERBERT LOM como El Capitán NEMO
Guión de JOHN PREBBLE, DANIEL ULLMAN y CRANE WILBUR
Efectos Visuales Especiales Creados por RAY HARRYHAUSEN
Dirigida por CY ENDFIELD • Un Film AMERAN
SUEVIA FILMS
COLUMBIA PICTURES INDUSTRIES, INC
Columbia Pictures

CHAPTER SEVEN **MYSTERIOUS ISLAND**

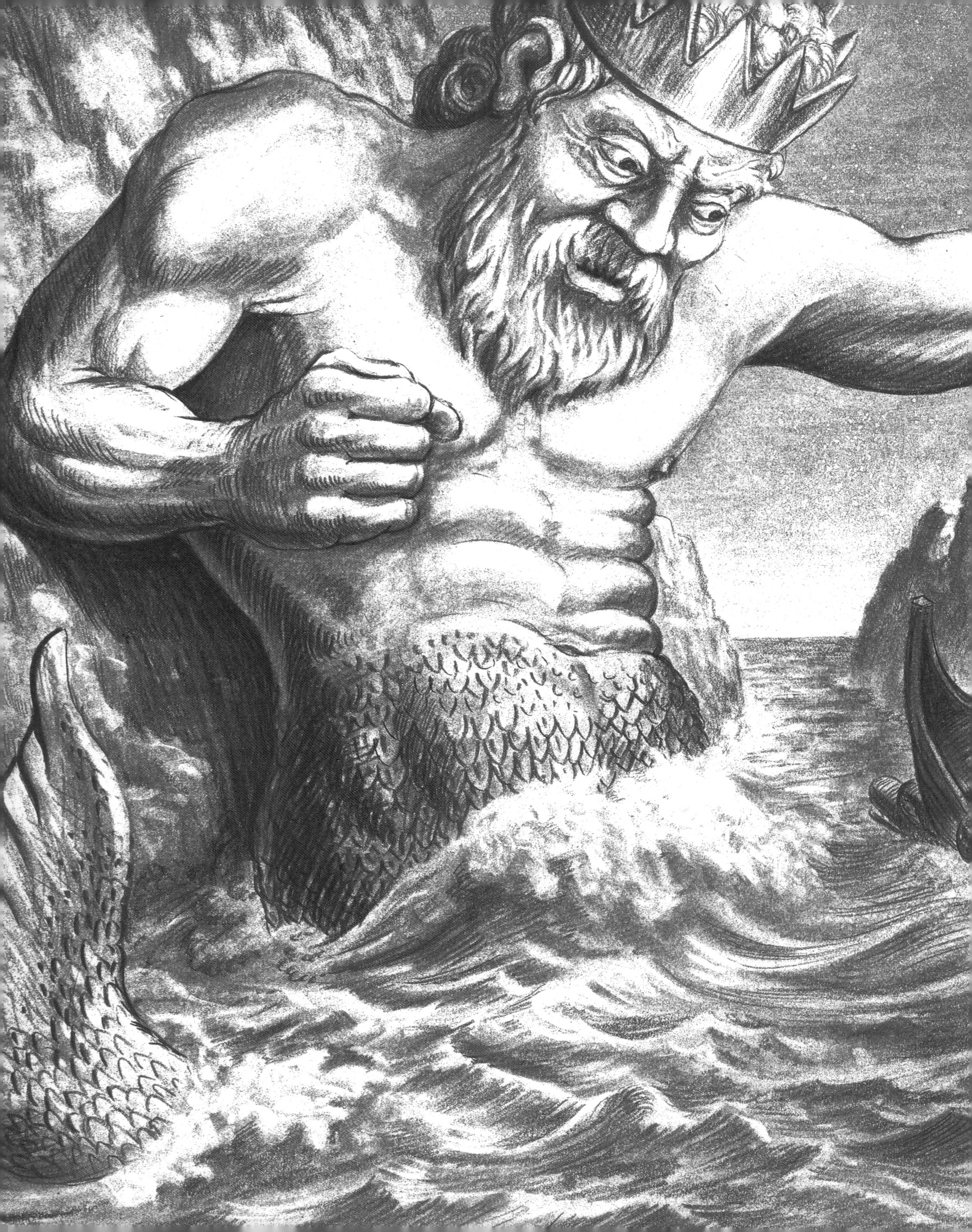

CHAPTER EIGHT

JASON AND THE ARGONAUTS (1963)

ASSOCIATE PRODUCER AND SPECIAL VISUAL EFFECTS: RAY HARRYHAUSEN

To claim back the kingdom of Thessaly, Jason and his crew of Argonauts set sail to the mysterious land of Colchis, in search of the Golden Fleece. But it's a voyage filled with many dangers. Arriving on the Isle of Bronze, their ship is destroyed by a giant living statue called Talos. Making good their escape, they offer assistance to a blind beggar called Phineas by helping him capture the gluttonous harpies. After a close shave with the deadly clashing rocks and the sea god, Triton, Jason rescues Medea, the beautiful High Priestess of Colchis, who shows him the way to the Fleece. But to obtain his prize, Jason must first battle with the seven-headed Hydra, and an army of skeletal warriors.

A COLOSSUS OF ADVENTURE!

Considered by many to be Ray's most accomplished film in realising the full potential of stop-motion animation, *Jason and the Argonauts* almost began life as another Sinbad adventure. With *The 7th Voyage of Sinbad* being such a financial success, Ray and Schneer felt certain that the name Sinbad was box-office gold. But the *Arabian Nights* gave way to Greek myths and legends, and so the hero of Ray's next film became Jason of Thessaly, whose ambition is to save his kingdom by acquiring the Golden Fleece from the mystical land of Colchis.

Jan Read (*First Men in the Moon*) was brought in by Schneer to write a script, although Beverley Cross (*Genghis Khan*) was employed to tie up all the loose ends so that scouting for locations and casting could begin. Budgeted at three million dollars, the film was a lot more costly than the last three color Dynamation movies put together.

Ray and Schneer considered Germany, Yugoslavia and Greece as suitable locations for live-action filming before finally settling on Southern Italy. The spectacular scenery of Palinuro was ideal for the beach scenes with the giant bronze statue, Talos, and the impressive temple ruins at Paestum provided the atmospheric backdrop to the scene in which blind beggar Phineas (Patrick Troughton) battles with the evil harpies.

The cast, as with *Mysterious Island*, was essentially British with the addition of little-known American actor Todd Armstrong in the lead. Dashing and heroic, he was the ideal choice, but like his glamorous co-star, American B-movie and theater actress Nancy

THIS PAGE: (Above) The skeleton fight scene at the film's climax took Ray over four months to animate. (Below) Instead of a stop-motion creature, Triton was played by Bill Gungeon.

HARRYHAUSEN THE MOVIE POSTERS

Kovack (who plays Medea), his accent jarred with the mainly British cast, so both he and Kovack were dubbed by other actors (Tim Turner and Eva Haddon respectively).

The rest of Jason's brave crew included Gary Raymond (*El Cid*) as Acastus, Andrew Faulds (*The Trollenberg Terror*) as Phalerus, Nigel Green (*Zulu*) as Hercules, and Laurence Naismith (*A Night to Remember*) as Argos the ship builder. Niall MacGinnis (*Night of the Demon*) played Zeus, king of the gods, and Honor Blackman (*Goldfinger*) his wife Hera.

With principal photography completed under the watchful eye of cinematographer Wilkie Cooper and the film's director Don Chaffey (*One Million Years B.C.*), Ray returned to Shepperton Studios outside London to start work on the Dynamation sequences. As with all his films to date, his father made the ball-and-socket armatures, over which Ray would weave his magic with layers of latex and colored paints. For sculptures of the creatures, Ray once again farmed out the work to Arthur Hayward at the Natural History Museum.

The first of Ray's stop-motion creatures to greet Jason and his crew on their long sea voyage to the land of Colchis is Talos, the merciless 300-feet-high 'living' bronze statue that crushes the Argonauts beneath its massive feet like a man stomping on an ant hill. Talos's first appearance is breathtaking and was inspired by the Colossus of Rhodes. The next menace to face the Argonauts are the bat-winged harpies, sinister flying creatures that swoop down to steal food. Ray used the aerial brace method to animate the harpies, in much the same way that he achieved the flying effect with the UFOs in *Earth Vs. the Flying Saucers*.

Jason's next challenge is to pass safely through the infamous clashing rocks, and he gets unexpected help from Triton, a giant merman who rises from the sea and pushes the titanic cliffs apart. Not a stop-motion figure, Triton was played by Canadian boxing champion Bill Gungeon, as Ray found that using a live actor was easier than dealing with the virtually impossible feat of filming water frame by frame! But even though it wasn't achieved through the Dynamation process, the sequence is still a highlight of the film given the extensive use of the sodium backing traveling matte system to place Jason and his crew into the very center of the maelstrom. The Columbia advertising department agreed and the image was extensively used as part of the film's poster campaign.

Perhaps Ray's finest work in this or any other of his movies is the double whammy he delivers at the climax of *Jason and the Argonauts*. First of all, in order to steal the Golden Fleece, Jason must kill the seven-headed Hydra that slithers from its cave dwelling, its snapping heads making it a formidable opponent. But when King Aeetes (Jack Gwillim) scatters the slain beast's teeth, they sprout seven life-size skeleton warriors armed with swords and shields.

Thanks to Ray's ability to breathe character into all his stop-motion figures, the skeletons in particular convey a distinct and lethal personality. The battle with Jason and his men takes up four and a half minutes of the film's running time, but the animation work took Ray four and a half months to complete, with every intricate movement of the skeletons carefully combined via Dynamation to the previously shot live action. And, as with Sinbad's sword fight in *The 7th Voyage of Sinbad*, the scene is further enhanced by Bernard Herrmann's evocative score.

Having taken nearly two years to complete, *Jason and the Argonauts* opened in America in June 1963. Two months later, in August, it made its UK debut on the Odeon cinema circuit where, doubling with Charles Schneer's British-made Arthurian adventure *Siege of the Saxons*, it quickly became one of the top-ten box office champions of the year. In fact it was so successful that Columbia re-released both films in time for the 1963 Christmas holidays and again during Easter 1964.

The British double-bill poster is particularly striking, with its sword-wielding warrior (Talos perhaps?) framing an image of Triton holding back the clashing rocks. The full UK quad, however, is disappointing. While it adopts similar artwork to the double-bill design, not a single one of the smaller pictures on the right-hand side of the poster showcases any of the Dynamation scenes.

Sadly the film wasn't as successful in America as it was in Europe. Released on a double-bill with an adventure set in ancient Rome called *Constantine and the Cross*, it was a combination of rather lackluster campaigning and cinema audiences' growing apathy to the Italian peblum movies that had swamped theaters during the early 1960s. It probably didn't help that another badly dubbed Italian movie called *Giants of Thessaly* was quickly released to cash in on the Harryhausen version and retitled *Jason and the Golden Fleece*. The film appeared on American television in 1966 and on the British commercial channel in 1971.

> **Jason and the Argonauts is considered to be Ray's most accomplished film in realising the full potential of stop-motion animation.**

Overseas posters tended to copy the American artwork, although artist Charles Rau's design for both the French and Belgian posters included Jason and his men. The 1978 re-release featured new artwork including a large image of Talos, while the UK's 1979 double-bill quad teamed it up with *Mysterious Island* and includes images of both the Hydra and the skeletons. Distributed on the Odeon circuit through the late seventies, it usually appeared alongside the low-budget *Star Wars* rip-off *The Humanoid* in order to cash in on the science fiction craze that was sweeping the nation.

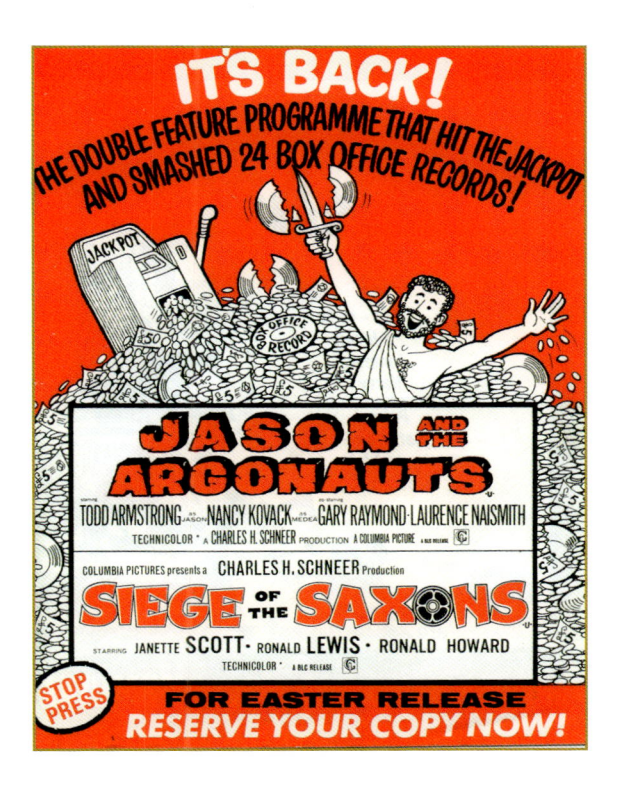

THIS PAGE: (Above) The double-bill release of *Jason and the Argonauts* and *Siege of the Saxons* broke box-office records across the British Isles.

CHAPTER EIGHT **JASON AND THE ARGONAUTS**

FOR THE FIRST TIME ON THE SCREEN!
THE EPIC STORY THAT WAS DESTINED TO STAND AS A COLOSSUS OF ADVENTURE!
COLUMBIA PICTURES presents A CHARLES H. SCHNEER PRODUCTION
JASON AND THE ARGONAUTS
starring
TODD ARMSTRONG · NANCY KOVACK · co-starring GARY RAYMOND · LAURENCE NAISMITH
as JASON
as MEDEA
Screenplay by JAN READ and BEVERLEY CROSS / Associate Producer RAY HARRYHAUSEN / Directed by DON CHAFFEY / A MORNINGSIDE WORLDWIDE FILM
EASTMAN COLOR
4048 COPYRIGHT © 1963 BY COLUMBIA PICTURES CORPORATION. ALL RIGHTS RESERVED. PRINTED IN U.S.A.

CHAPTER EIGHT **JASON AND THE ARGONAUTS**

HARRYHAUSEN THE MOVIE POSTERS

PREVIOUS SPREAD: PAGE 106 US One-sheet (69 x 104cm) Courtesy of Simon Greetham Archive.
PAGE 107 French Grande (115 x 157cm) Art by Charles Rau.

THIS SPREAD: (Left) British Quad (76 x 102cm) Courtesy of Mark Mawston Archive. (Above) Belgian (36 x 48cm) Courtesy of Mike Hankin Archive.

CHAPTER EIGHT **JASON AND THE ARGONAUTS** 109

HARRYHAUSEN THE MOVIE POSTERS

THIS SPREAD: (Left) US Half-sheet (56 x 71cm) Art by G Meyer. (Above) Finnish (40 x 60cm) Art by R Kanz. Courtesy of eMoviePoster.com/Hershenson/Allen Archive.

NEXT SPREAD: PAGE 112 (Top Left) French Grande (115 x 157cm) Art by E.A. Ubis. Courtesy of Ray Harryhausen Archive. (Top Right) Italian 2 Fogli (99 x 140cm) Art by M. Copizzi. (Bottom) British Quad (76 x 102cm) Courtesy of Simon Greetham Archive. PAGE 113 US (101 x 152cm) Courtesy of eMoviePoster.com/Hershenson/Allen Archive.

CHAPTER EIGHT **JASON AND THE ARGONAUTS**

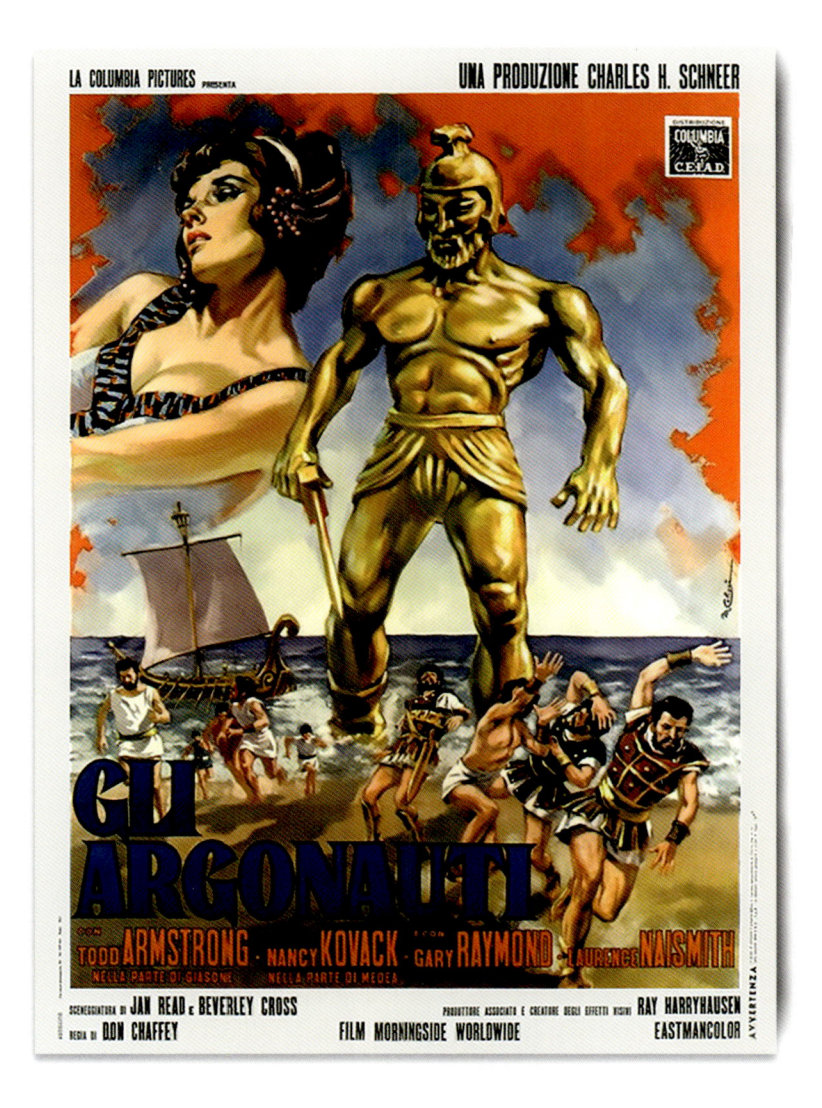

HARRYHAUSEN THE MOVIE POSTERS

CHAPTER EIGHT **JASON AND THE ARGONAUTS**

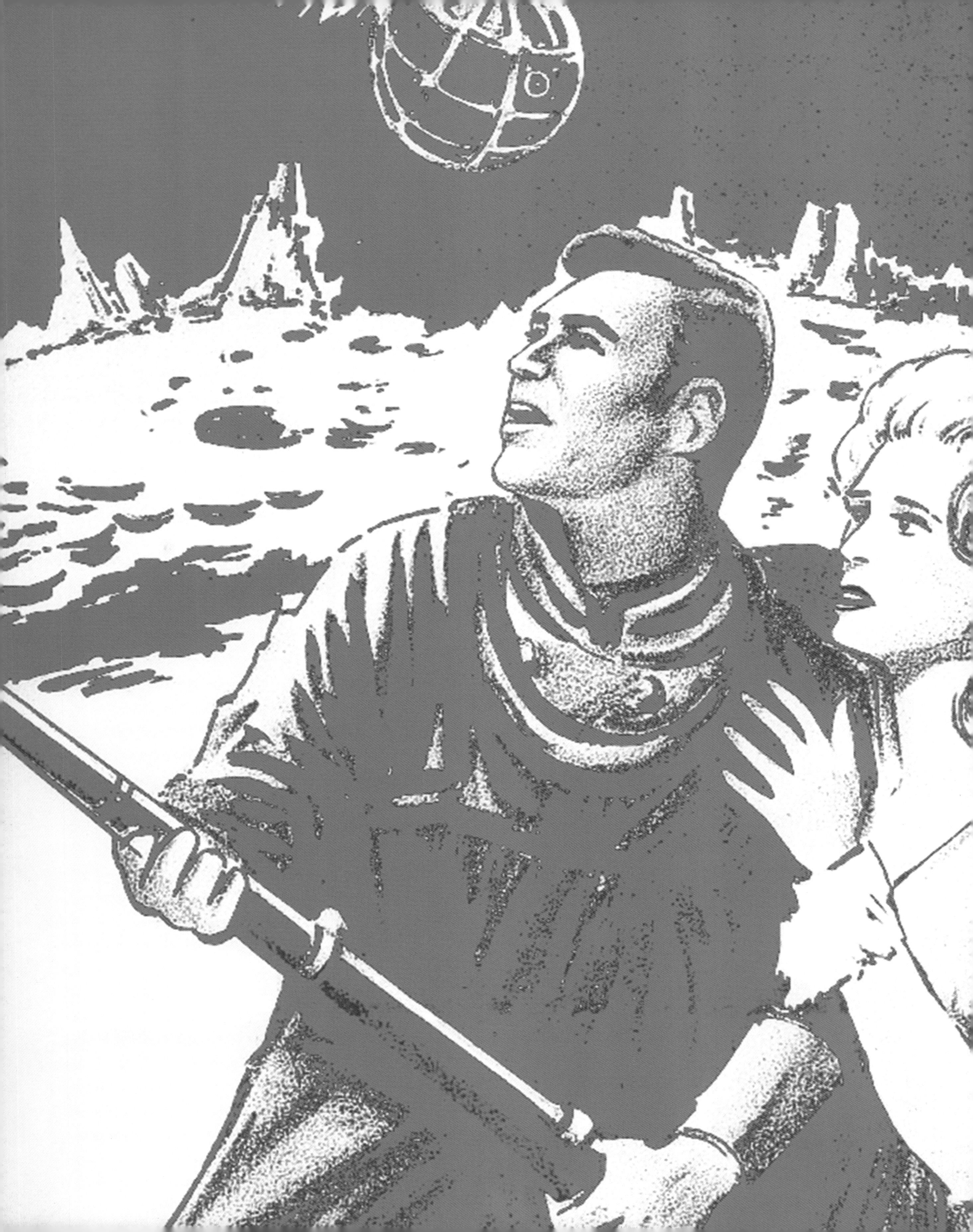

CHAPTER NINE

FIRST MEN IN THE MOON (1964)

ASSOCIATE PRODUCER AND SPECIAL VISUAL EFFECTS: RAY HARRYHAUSEN

While exploring the lunar surface, the crew of a United Nations spacecraft discovers a faded British flag. This turns out to be the property of an eccentric scientist called Professor Cavor, who 65 years earlier had visited the Moon in an anti-gravity sphere, along with his business partner Arnold Bedford, and Bedford's fiancée Kate Callender. Unfortunately, the Selenites, the insect-like creatures who lived beneath the lunar surface, suspected that the human visitors were actually the vanguard of a full-scale invasion. In order to placate them, Cavor agreed to remain on the Moon, while his two traveling companions escaped back to Earth. When the United Nations astronauts find the Selenites' underground city, they discover that a cold virus that Cavor had unwittingly taken with him to the Moon has wiped out the entire civilization.

BEYOND THE LIMITS OF IMAGINATION!

Having already brought Jules Verne's novel *The Mysterious Island* to the screen in 1961, Ray turned to another science fiction author for his next project. A devotee of the works of H.G. Wells, Ray suggested to his business partner Charles Schneer that they film an adaptation of Wells' 1901 novel, *The First Men in the Moon*.

At first, Schneer was dubious about the idea, believing that period pictures were not always successful at the box office, but agreed to commission science fiction author Nigel Kneale to write the screenplay. Kneale, who was the creator of the phenomenally successful *Quatermass* television serials, remained faithful to the Victorian setting but, with the Apollo Moon landings a certainty by the close of the decade, concocted a modern prologue to act as a framework for the story.

In Kneale's final version of the script, the story of the Victorian astronauts' voyage into space and their encounter with the Selenites (the creatures that inhabit the Moon) would be told in flashback. Ray and Schneer were delighted with the idea, but Columbia wanted a love interest to appeal to audiences, and insisted that the Victorian astronauts took a female companion with them. Disappointed with the alterations to his script, Kneale bowed out and so Jan Read, who had co-written *Jason and the Argonauts*, was brought in to tweak the story to include a woman. The title *First 'Men' in the Moon*, however, was left unchanged.

THIS PAGE: (Above) Due to the incompatability of Ray's Dynamation process with Panavision, the majority of the Selenites were played by child actors in costume. (Below) The amazing full-size moon sphere created by Ray and production designer John Blezard.

HARRYHAUSEN THE MOVIE POSTERS

The key problem for Ray was Schneer's decision to shoot the film in Panavision, a popular widescreen system that was first introduced in the 1950s. For Panavision to work, a film would be shot using an anamorphic lens, which squeezed a widescreen image onto 35mm film, and then a similar device fitted to a projector would reverse the procedure in the cinema. The trouble was, the anamorphic system wasn't compatible with Dynamation and created serious lighting problems with the stop-motion back projection. Complications with using Panavision also negated the use of the sodium vapor system, which had proved so successful in combining the live-action and miniature elements in both *Mysterious Island* and *Jason and the Argonauts*. The only answer was to use blue screen, which was less effective and prone to fringing, while the rest of the film's special effects were created via traveling mattes or split-screen, with Ray's stop-motion animation reduced to less than five minutes in the finished film.

As a result, Ray's Selenites (articulated nine-inch-high models that captured Wells' original depiction of a strange race of insectoid-type creatures) are used very sparingly. Child actors in rubber suits were hired to play the rest of the lunar population. The film does include a giant stop-motion moonbeast, which proved time-consuming to animate due to its caterpillar-like body and hundreds of tiny legs.

The film's cast included Edward Judd (*The Day the Earth Caught Fire*) as Arnold Bedford, the self-obsessed but failed entrepreneur who agrees to travel to the Moon for purely monetary gains, and Lionel Jeffries (*Chitty Chitty Bang Bang*) in the role of Professor Cavor, a character who combined the genius of Albert Einstein with the eccentricity of W. Heath Robinson. American Martha Hyer (*Pyro*) played the love interest, Kate Callander, Bedford's fiancé and reluctant astronaut.

Nathan Juran returned to the Harryhausen/Schneer camp for the third and last time as director, and deserves much credit for turning this low-budget movie into something of a widescreen epic. Juran's background as an art director came to the fore throughout, and Ray always considered him one of the few directors that 'understood' what was required in a special effects-laden movie, such as *First Men in the Moon*.

The construction of the lunar surface on the enormous H Stage at Shepperton Studios adds to the overall grandeur of the film. The mountainous terrain, with its giant craters and towering peaks, is far more dramatic looking than the flat sun-lit horizon that welcomed the *Apollo II* astronauts six years later. Locations close to the studio also provided authentic period settings, including Bedford's picturesque cottage, while an imposing country house near Reading in Berkshire providing the perfect setting for Cavor's laboratory.

Ray and the film's production designer John Blezard designed the sphere, the anti-gravity spacecraft that transports Cavor and his companions to the Moon. Based on Wells' description, Ray covered the outer skin with railway bumpers in order to shield its occupants from the shock of tumbling across the lunar surface. Models of the sphere were constructed for the scenes set in outer space, while a full-sized, one-ton version made of wood and fibreglass was used for the live-action sequences. The sphere's interior, with its plush red velvet lining and Victorian trimmings, was built on an adjacent set.

With less of his traditional stop-motion methods needed in the film, Ray spent considerable time working at Les Bowie's special effects facility in Slough. Schneer was delighted by the cut-price but totally believable work that Bowie had provided for sections of both *Mysterious Island* and *Jason and the Argonauts*, so while Ray honed the animation, Bowie and his small team of technicians constructed detailed miniatures of the Moon's surface and the greenhouse that loses its roof when Cavor's anti-gravity paint Cavorite reaches its critical state and catapults the sphere 'at the speed of a bullet' into deep space (this scene was actually shot with the miniature greenhouse suspended upside down to simulate the effect of debris being hurled upwards). Principal photography took twelve weeks to complete, while the post-production stage lasted for seven months. Previously shot footage of the actors moving in front of blue screens, as they tour through the wonders of the Selenite world, were perfectly matched to the miniature sets at Slough through the use of traveling mattes.

A disagreement over finances meant that Bernard Hermann wasn't available to score the movie, so the task fell to Laurie Johnson (*The Avengers*), who had written the music for Schneer's medieval adventure *Siege of the Saxons* (the supporting feature with *Jason and the Argonauts*). Johnson's score is both melodic and atmospheric, with orchestral lushness in scenes such as the entrance to the hall of the Grand Lunar. Johnson also wrote the score for the film's companion picture, period adventure *East of Sudan*.

First Men in the Moon premiered in London on August 6th 1964 at the Plaza Theatre and went on general release on a double-bill with *East of Sudan* on the Odeon cinema circuit from August 16th. It was reissued on August 1st 1969 as a supporting feature to the children's drama *Run Wild Run Free*. Two years later (in 1971), the film made its commercial television debut in the UK.

The film opened in America in November 1964, with one magazine critic commenting, "It is Ray Harryhausen's amazing and terrifying special effects which are the real stars here." Columbia's advertising campaign included an endorsement by NASA and a tie-in display at Macy's Thanksgiving Day Parade. But the film's popularity in America was rather muted with little or no merchandise, apart from a Gold Key comic book, a tie-in novelization and a promotion with Revell model kits.

While the majority of the overseas posters reused the American artwork, the UK campaign opted for a larger image of the film's main stars against a drawing of the Grand Lunar's cavern. This image was redrawn for the double-bill poster with *East of Sudan*. As with the American release, merchandise in the UK was restricted to a paperback tie-in from Fontana Books and a magazine competition in the Odeon's *Showtime* magazine.

Being more liberally-minded in Europe, French poster artist Roger Soubie's painting for the film features Martha Hyer sitting on top of the sphere without the protection of a space helmet, while her traveling companions hop around the lunar surface in their customised diving suits.

THIS PAGE: (Above) Martha Hyer comes face to face with a Selenite.

CHAPTER NINE **FIRST MEN IN THE MOON**

H.G. WELLS' ASTOUNDING ADVENTURE IN
DYNAMATION!
COLUMBIA PICTURES
presents a
CHARLES H.
SCHNEER
production
H.G.WELLS'
FIRST MEN IN THE MOON
IN PANAVISION · LUNACOLOR · DYNAMATION
starring
EDWARD JUDD · MARTHA HYER and LIONEL JEFFRIES · Screenplay by NIGEL KNEALE and JAN READ
Associate Producer RAY HARRYHAUSEN · Directed by NATHAN JURAN · AN AMERAN FILM
FIRST MAN IN THE MOON
64-347

CHAPTER NINE **FIRST MEN IN THE MOON**

HARRYHAUSEN THE MOVIE POSTERS

PREVIOUS SPREAD: PAGE 119 US (101 x 152cm) Courtesy of Ray Harryhausen Archive. PAGE 120 French Grande (115 x 157cm) Art by Roger Soubie. Courtesy of Neil Pettigrew Archive.

THIS SPREAD: (Left) US Half-sheet (56 x 71cm) Courtesy of Andy Johnson Archive. (Above) US Insert (36 x 91cm) Courtesy of Simon Greetham Archive.

CHAPTER NINE **FIRST MEN IN THE MOON**

THIS SPREAD: British Quad (76 x 102cm) Courtesy of Simon Greetham Archive.

122 HARRYHAUSEN THE MOVIE POSTERS

CHAPTER NINE **FIRST MEN IN THE MOON**

124

HARRYHAUSEN THE MOVIE POSTERS

THIS SPREAD: (Far Left) German A1 (58 x 84cm) Courtesy of Neil Pettigrew Archive. (Left) Italian Locandina (35 x 68cm). (Above) Danish (62 x 84cm) Courtesy of eMoviePoster.com/Hershenson/Allen Archive.

CHAPTER NINE **FIRST MEN IN THE MOON** 125

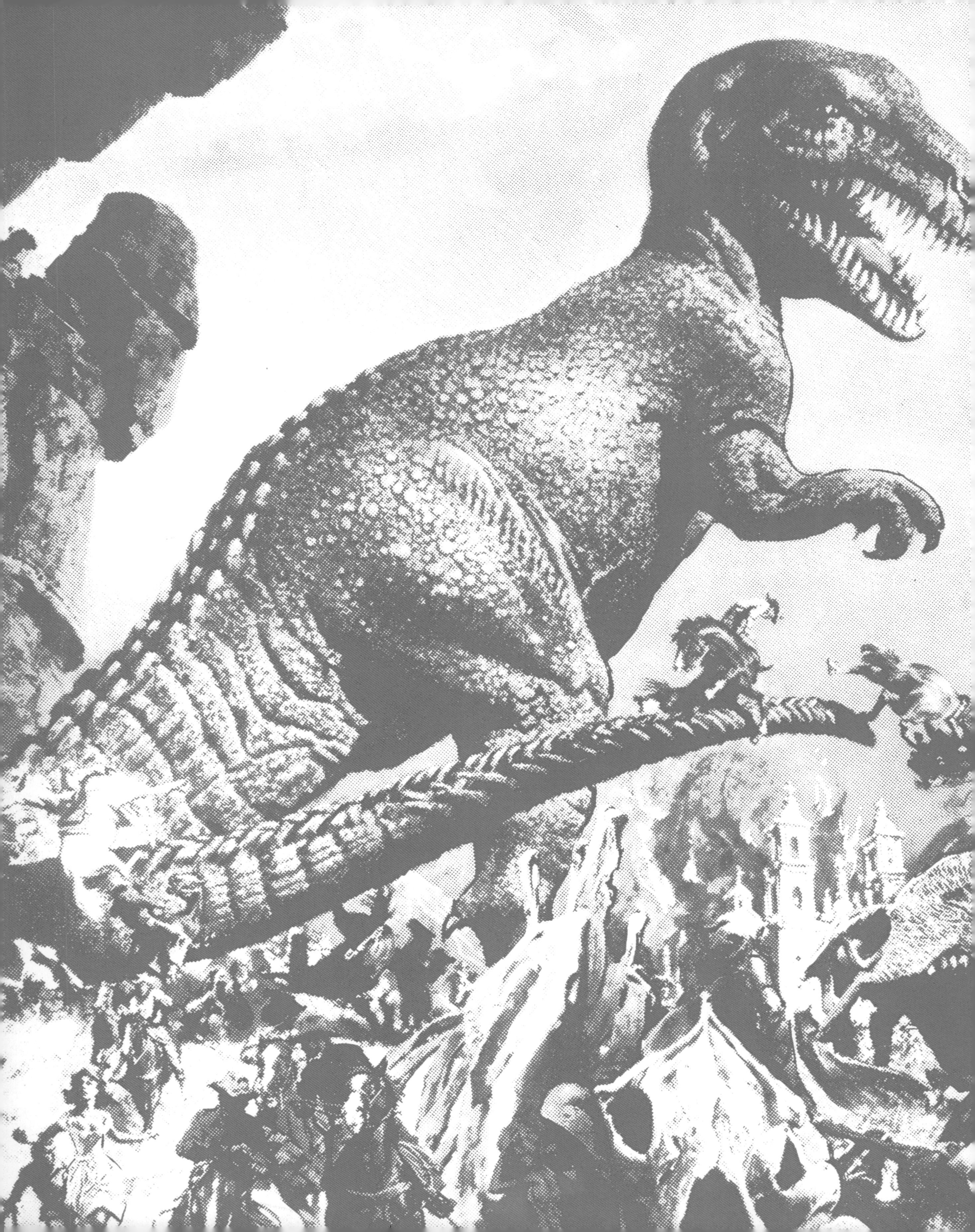

CHAPTER TEN

ONE MILLION YEARS BC (1966) THE VALLEY OF GWANGI (1969)

SPECIAL VISUAL EFFECTS: RAY HARRYHAUSEN (*ONE MILLION YEARS B.C.*)
ASSOCIATE PRODUCER AND VISUAL EFFECTS: RAY HARRYHAUSEN (*THE VALLEY OF GWANGI*)

ONE MILLION YEARS B.C.: In a strange prehistoric world where early man co-exists with dinosaurs, two opposing tribes are brought together by the relationship between the beautiful Loana of the Shell People and the grizzled Tumak, whose Rock tribe live in the mountains. But their ancient world is fraught with dangers, including an attack by a flesh-eating allosaurus, a ferocious battle between two prehistoric titans and a cataclysmic volcanic eruption. Other perils include Loana being carried off by a giant flying reptile, and a nail-biting escape from the clutches of a tribe of cannibals.

THE VALLEY OF GWANGI: Looking for more audience-grabbing attractions, the owners of a travelling Wild West show hear of a legend about a giant creature that lives in a lost valley in Mexico. Finding the hidden entrance, they are amazed to discover that the valley is the home to many different species of dinosaur. After numerous encounters with a flying reptile and a horned styracosaurus, the cowboys capture a tyrannosaurus, which the local Indians call Gwangi. But taking their captive back to civilization ends in disaster when Gwangi escapes, kills a circus elephant and chases the heroes into a large cathedral. When the cathedral catches fire, Gwangi perishes in the flames.

CREATURES OF A LOST ERA!
100 MILLION YEARS B.C.

Having worked exclusively with Charles Schneer since their first feature film together in 1955 (the only exception being *The Animal World* in 1956), Ray took a break from their successful partnership at Morningside Productions and accepted an invitation from Seven Arts and Hammer Films to provide the stop-motion effects for its 1966 color remake of an old Hal Roach movie combining dinosaurs and cavemen called *One Million B.C.* (1940).

One Million Years B.C., as it was retitled, was Hammer's 100th film and also its most expensive (£425,000). Once on board the project, Ray assigned Arthur Hayward to sculpt the prehistoric animals from his preliminary sketches. The dinosaurs that Ray chose for the film included an enormous sea turtle, a predatory allosaurus, a flesh-eating ceratosaurus, a three-horned triceratops and a pteranodon with the wingspan of a small plane. Ray also built a brontosaurus for an intended scene in which it attacks the human stars of the film, but both financial and time constraints meant that the dinosaur was relegated to a distant cameo shot.

Ray spent eight months working on the stop-motion sequences at ABPC Elstree Studios, highlights of which included a battle to the death between the ceratosaurus and the triceratops, and a ferocious attack by the allosaurus. One complicated scene to

THIS PAGE: (Above) Ray's pre-production drawing of the allosaurus attacking the camp of the Shell tribe. (Below) The scene as it appears set up for Ray's rear-projection system with the stop-motion model in the foreground.

128 HARRYHAUSEN THE MOVIE POSTERS

animate, for which Ray reused the aerial brace method of suspending his models on wires, required his pterodactyl model to swoop down and fly away with one of the stars of the film clasped firmly in its claws.

Wilkie Cooper returned to handle the cinematography, and Don Chaffey once again took up the assignment as director. Les Bowie was also brought in by Ray and Schneer to handle some of the miniature effects, glass paintings and a lengthy prologue that showed the creation of the world. As always, Bowie and his team performed cinematic miracles, producing the convincing special effects (including an earthquake and exploding volcano) on a minuscule budget.

Because the film's dialogue is made up of a succession of neanderthal-like grunts befitting a prehistoric tribe, actors for the leading roles in the film were selected more for their appearance than their acting ability. Raquel Welch (*Fantastic Voyage*) was chosen to play the glamorous Luana, a member of the peace-loving Shell Tribe. Welch proved an ideal asset for the movie as her shapely fur bikini-clad figure dominated the film's advertising campaign.

Welch's co-star was John Richardson (*Tumak*), who had starred opposite Ursula Andress in the Hammer version of *She* the year before. With his strong masculine appearance and piercing blue eyes he was the perfect screen partner for the voluptuous Welch. The supporting cast was selected from a host of British actors, including Percy Herbert (*Mysterious Island*) as the villainous Sakana, Robert Brown (M in the Bond movies) as the tribe's patriarch Akhoba, and Martine Beswick (*Thunderball*) as Nupondi, who challenges Luana to a raunchy cat fight over Tumak's affections.

Mario Nascimbene (*When Dinosaurs Ruled the Earth*) provided both the film's musical score and sound effects, using a combination of orchestral instruments, voices and electronic sounds.

The Canary Islands, in particular Lanzarote with its rugged volcanic terrain, provided a suitable backdrop for the desolate landscape of the Rock Tribe. Interiors for the film were shot some weeks later on two large sets constructed at the ABPC Elstree Studios outside London.

One Million Years B.C. opened in Britain in December 1966, and toured the ABC cinema circuit on a double-bill with *The Bugs Bunny Show No 5*, making it one of the distributors' top ten box office attractions for the year. Given an A certificate in the UK, it was released uncut — although the American version was slightly edited for violence. The film opened in America in February 1967, with bylines such as 'Discover a savage world whose only law is lust!' and toured with a wartime drama called *I Deal in Danger*.

Raquel Welch's appearance on the film's poster art, by artists Tom Chantrell (UK) and Jack Thurston (USA), dominated the publicity for *One Million Years B.C.*. Thanks to a combination of this image and Ray's amazing special effects, the film proved to be a huge money-spinner for Hammer, grossing over two million pounds in the UK and a total of eight million dollars worldwide.

In Japan, the publicity for the film underplayed the Welch connection in favour of the dinosaurs. But some of the alternative artwork promoted the damsel-in-distress theme, reproducing Thurston's artwork of Loana in the grasping claws of a pteranodon, with the byline, 'Beauty in the jaws of the beast!'

One Million Years B.C. had a major cinema re-release on the ABC cinema circuit in August 1969, and appeared on American television for the first time in 1970 (premiering on BBC television in 1974). For the late sixties re-release, in which it shared a double-bill with Hammer's film version of *She*, the studio produced another stunning poster design, with Welch standing alongside Ursula Andress.

THIS PAGE: (Left) Cover of the *ABC Film Review* magazine. (Above) Raquel Welch and John Richardson attend the promotional launch of the film.

CHAPTER TEN **ONE MILLION YEARS BC**

HARRYHAUSEN THE MOVIE POSTERS

CHAPTER TEN **ONE MILLION YEARS BC**

HARRYHAUSEN THE MOVIE POSTERS

PREVIOUS SPREAD: PAGE 130 US One-sheet (69 x 104cm) Art by Jack Thurston. Courtesy of Neil Pettigrew Archive. PAGE 131 Spanish (70 x 99cm) Art by Jack Thurston. Courtesy of Mark Mawston Archive.

THIS SPREAD: (Left) British Quad (76 x 102cm) Art by Tom Chantrell. Courtesy of Ray Harryhausen Archive. (Above) US Insert (36 x 91cm) Art by Jack Thurston.

NEXT SPREAD: PAGE 134: (Clockwise from top left) Polish (58 x 83cm) Art by Bodham Butenko. Belgian (36 x 48cm) Art by Paul Tamin. Yugoslavian (48 x 69cm). Spanish (70 x 99cm) Art by Enrique Mataix. Courtesy of Neil Pettigrew Archive. PAGE 135: Italian 2 Fogli (99 x 140cm).

CHAPTER TEN **ONE MILLION YEARS BC** 133

HARRYHAUSEN THE MOVIE POSTERS

CHAPTER TEN **ONE MILLION YEARS BC**

HARRYHAUSEN THE MOVIE POSTERS

CHAPTER TEN **ONE MILLION YEARS BC**

HAMMER GLAMOUR ! HAMME
RAQUEL
WELCH
ONE
MILLION
YEARS B.C.
TECHNICOLOR
A
ASSOCIATED BRITISH PATHE present A HAMMER FILM PRODUCTION
ONE MILLION YEARS B.C. A
STARRING
RAQUEL WELCH · JOHN RICHARDSON
with
PERCY HERBERT · ROBERT BROWN
MARTINE BESWICK
ASSOCIATED BRITISH presents A HAMMER FILM PRODUCTION
URSULA ANDRESS as

PREVIOUS SPREAD: PAGE 136 Japanese B2 (51 x 76cm).
PAGE 137 Japanese B2 (51 x 76cm).

THIS SPREAD: British Quad (76 x 102cm)
Courtesy of Andy Johnson Archive.

CHAPTER TEN **ONE MILLION YEARS BC**

THE VALLEY OF GWANGI

With the success of *One Million Years B.C.* and the public's growing fascination for dinosaurs, Ray showed Charles Schneer sketches for an aborted Willis O'Brien project about a dinosaur being captured by a Wild West show. Convinced that such a combination would be a surefire winner at the box office, Schneer engaged Julian More (*Incense for the Damned*) and veteran television writer William Bast to develop a new screenplay from O'Brien's original. The producer then took the script, now called *The Valley of Gwangi*, to Warner Bros—Seven Arts (Hammer's partners on *One Million Years B.C.*). Enthused by the idea, they immediately offered up the necessary finance.

Popular leading man James Franciscus (*Beneath the Planet of the Apes*) was cast in the lead as the hero Tuck Kirby, with Polish actress Gila Golan (*Ship of Fools*) playing his feisty girlfriend, T.J. Breckenridge. The supporting cast included American Richard Carlson (*It Came From Outer Space*) as Champ Connors, and British stalwarts Freda Jackson (*Clash of the Titans*) in the role of the gypsy Tia Zorina, and Laurence Naismith (*Jason and the Argonauts*) as the eccentric paleontologist Professor Bromley.

The film was directed by James O'Connolly (*The Hi-Jackers*), while the cinematography was handled by Erwin Hillier (*The Dambusters*). Jerome Moross (*The Big Country*) wrote the film score, which went a long way to underpin the film's Western theme.

THIS PAGE: (Above) The fight between Gwangi and the styracosaurus as Ray envisaged it in the pre-production stage. (Below) The scene as it appears in the film.

140 HARRYHAUSEN THE MOVIE POSTERS

Spain (Almeria and Cuena) was once again used for filming, this time doubling as Mexico, although the interiors were shot in a television studio in Madrid and at the Cathedral of Cuencas respectively (the impressive location for the film's fiery climax). The unusual landscape of Ciudad Encantada doubled for the Forbidden Valley, a lost world in which dinosaurs still roamed.

After the live action was completed, Ray set to work on the stop-motion animation at his custom-built workshop in Shepperton Studios. Among the dinosaurs included in the film, again sculpted by Arthur Hayward of the Natural History Museum, was the eponymous hero Gwangi, a sort of cross between a tyrannosaurus and an allosaurus (the dinosaur that had attacked the village of the shell people in *One Million Years B.C.*). There was also an eohippus (miniature horse), a pterodactyl, a horned dinosaur called a styracosaurus, a bird-like reptile known as an ornithomimus and a modern-day elephant.

The most remarkable feature about the stop-motion sections of the film is just how much Ray integrates his creatures with the live action. Placing humans and models convincingly in the same scene had always been one of Ray's specialties, and *The Valley of Gwangi* is full of such sequences, including a young boy called Lope (Curtis Arden) being plucked into the air by a pterodactyl (a la Raquel Welch in *One Million Years B.C.*); Gwangi being towed in a makeshift cage by cowboys on horseback; and in one of the most impressive examples of Ray's Dynamation process, Gwangi being lassoed by cowboys in a scene that first required the live-action filming of a moving jeep fitted with a wooden pole 4.5 meters high, and then five months of complex stop-motion animation. All in all *The Valley of Gwangi* included 400 stop-motion cuts and the herculean task of animating all the creatures took Ray almost a year to complete.

The Valley of Gwangi opened in America in September 1969, on a double-bill with a comedy called *Seven Golden Men* and the following month at the New Victoria Cinema in London. It went on general release on the ABC circuit from November 23rd, but due to changes at Warner Brothers the new management at Seven Arts expressed little interest in the film, relegating it to a supporting feature on a double-bill with the comedy western *The Good Guys and the Bad Guys*. As a result the film fared badly at the box office.

The UK double-bill poster is very uninspiring with two-tone coloring. The full quad for the film, on the other hand, is the complete opposite with a spectacular painting by Frank McCarthy (1924–2002) showing a Godzilla-sized Gwangi surrounded by fleeing horseback riders. This same artwork appeared on all of the American posters, and a large number of the international campaigns.

For the Belgian release of the film, the image was adapted by artist Raymond Elseviers to give it a more ethereal appearance (*La Vallée Des Monstres*), while Italian poster artist Picchioni Franco (1942–2002) gave greater prominence to the film's human stars, Franciscus and Golan (*La Vendetta Di Gwangi*). Franco's alternative poster version featured a very different design for Gwangi, turning him into a green-colored lizard that looks nothing like the film's stop-motion star.

Campaign material aside, merchandise for the movie was scant, with a tie-in comic book being the most accessible item. The film was never re-released, and made its UK television debut in 1974.

THIS PAGE: (Left) In 1969, Ray (seen here holding the model of Gwangi) visited the ABC cinema in Glasgow as part of the promotional tour. (Top Right) At the climax of the film Gwangi storms the cathedral. (Bottom Right) The staff of the ABC Cinema in Catford, South London help to promote the film.

CHAPTER TEN **THE VALLEY OF GWANGI**

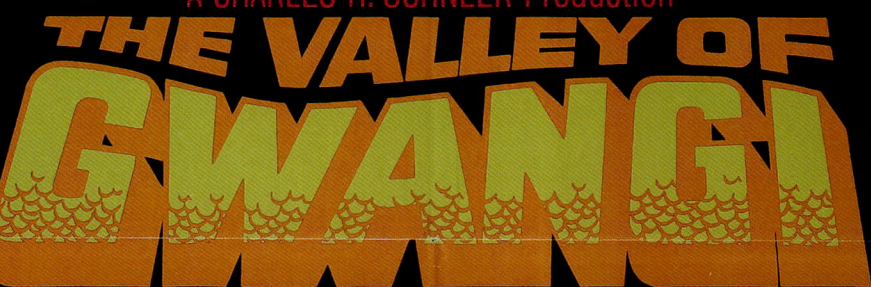

HARRYHAUSEN THE MOVIE POSTERS

CHAPTER TEN **THE VALLEY OF GWANGI**

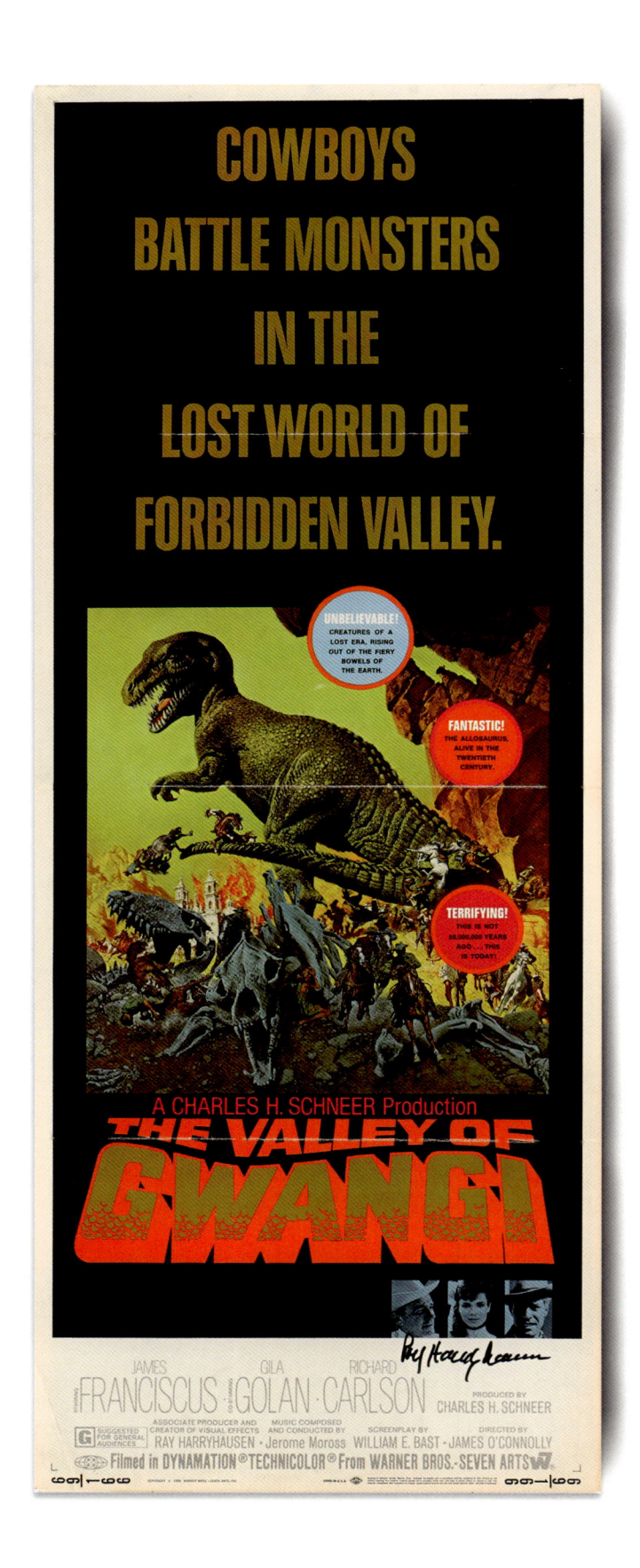

PREVIOUS SPREAD: PAGE 142 US One-sheet (69 x 104cm) Art by Frank McCarthy. Courtesy of Neil Pettigrew Archive. PAGE 143 French Grande (115 x 157cm) Art by Frank McCarthy. Courtesy of Ray Harryhausen Archive.

THIS SPREAD: (Above) US Insert (36 x 91cm) Art by Frank McCarthy. Courtesy of Andy Johnson Archive. (Top Right) German A1 (58 x 84cm) Art by Frank McCarthy. Courtesy of Andy Johnson Archive. (Bottom Right) British Double Crown (51 x 69cm) Courtesy of eMoviePoster.com/Hershenson/Allen Archive. (Opposite) Italian 2 Fogli (99 x 140cm).

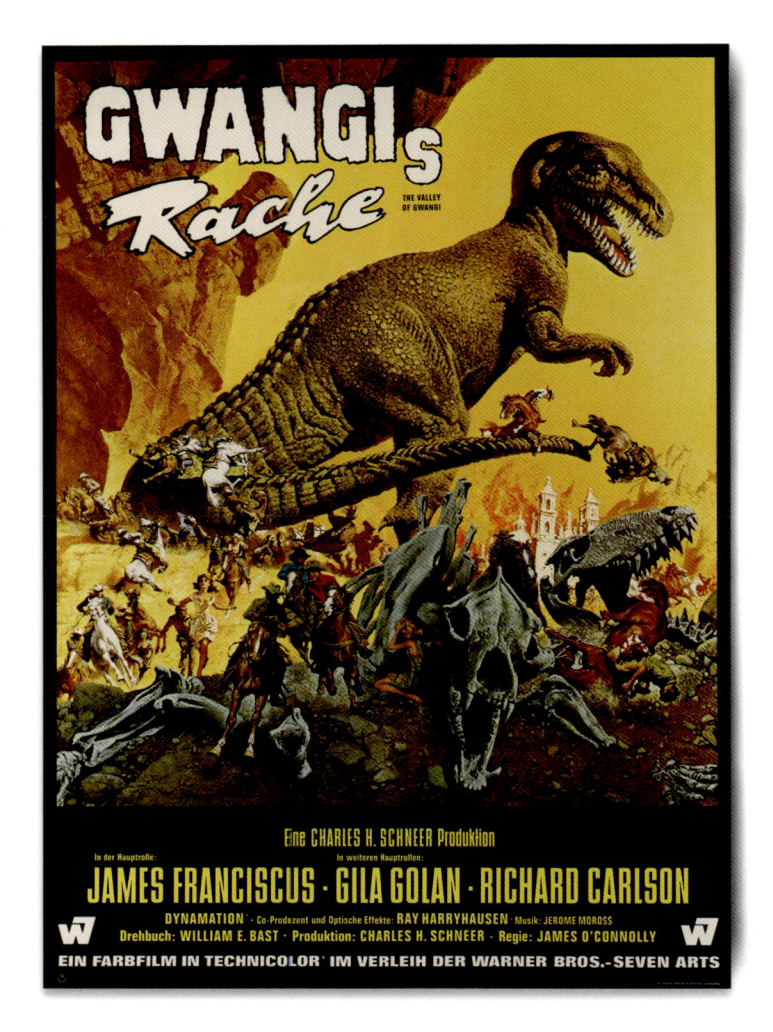

144 HARRYHAUSEN THE MOVIE POSTERS

CHAPTER TEN **THE VALLEY OF GWANGI**

HARRYHAUSEN THE MOVIE POSTERS

CHAPTER TEN **THE VALLEY OF GWANGI**

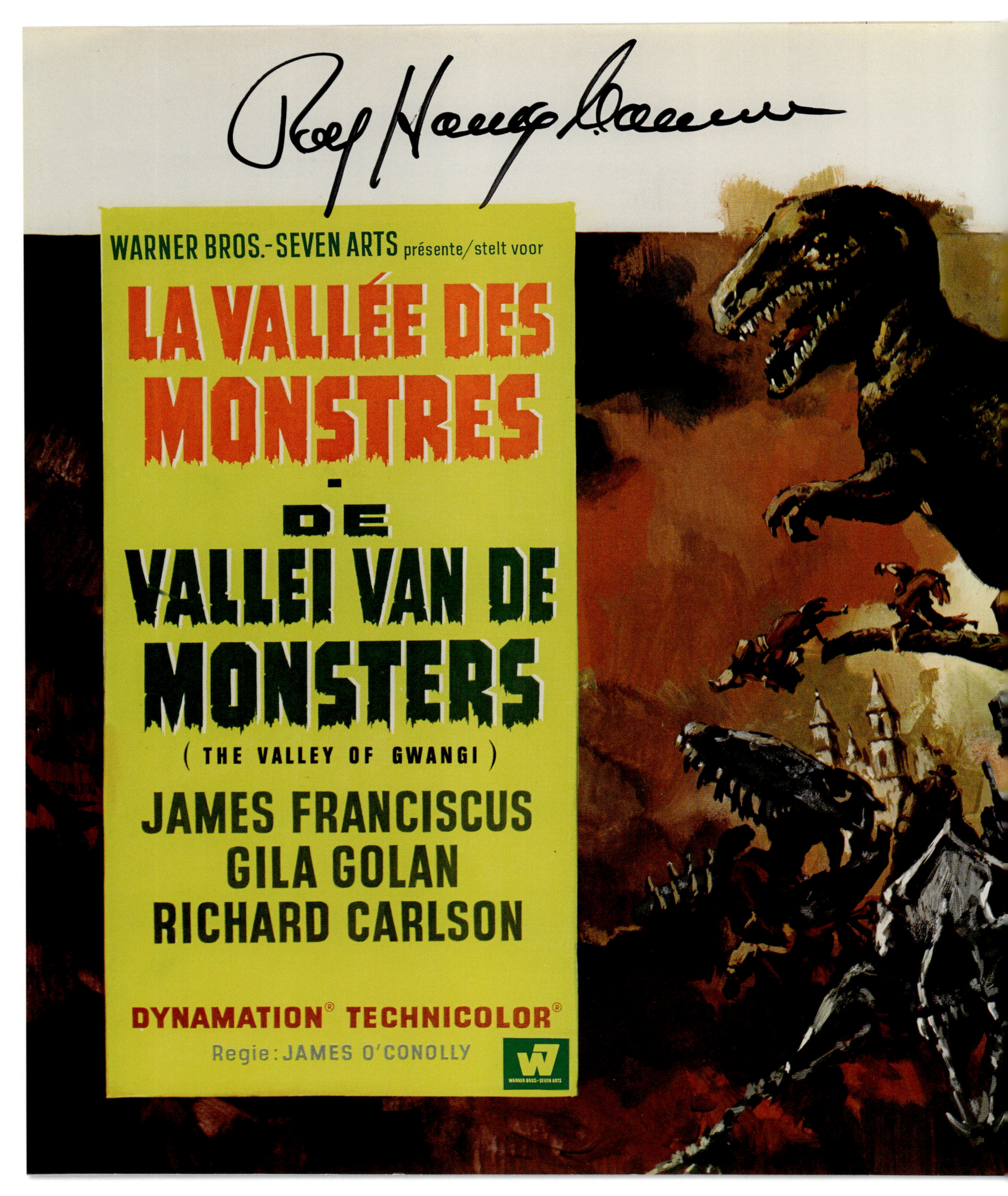

HARRYHAUSEN THE MOVIE POSTERS

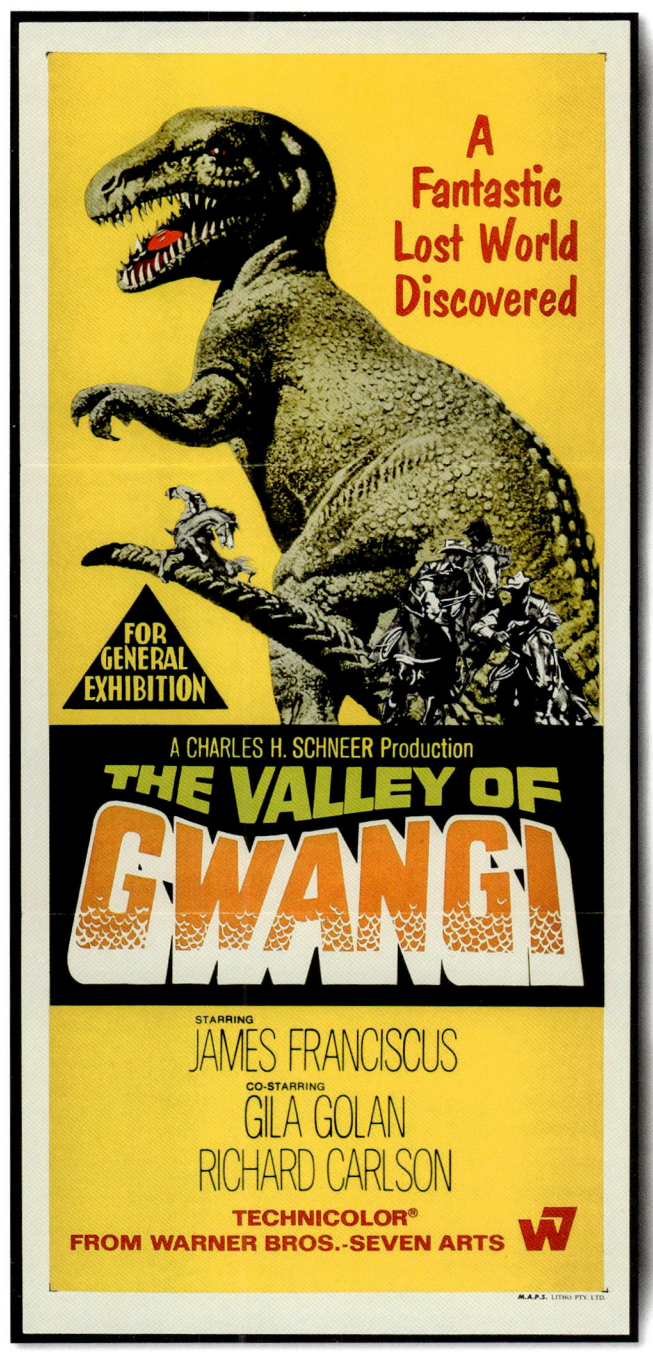

PREVIOUS SPREAD: PAGE 146 Italian 2 Fogli (99 x 140cm) Art by Franco Picchioni. Courtesy of Neil Pettigrew Archive. PAGE 147 Japanese B2 (51 x 76cm) Art by Frank McCarthy. Courtesy of Mark Mawston Archive.

THIS SPREAD: (Left) Belgian (36 x 48cm) Art by Raymond Elseviers. Courtesy of Andy Johnson Archive. (Above) Australian Daybill (34 x 77cm)

CHAPTER TEN **THE VALLEY OF GWANGI**

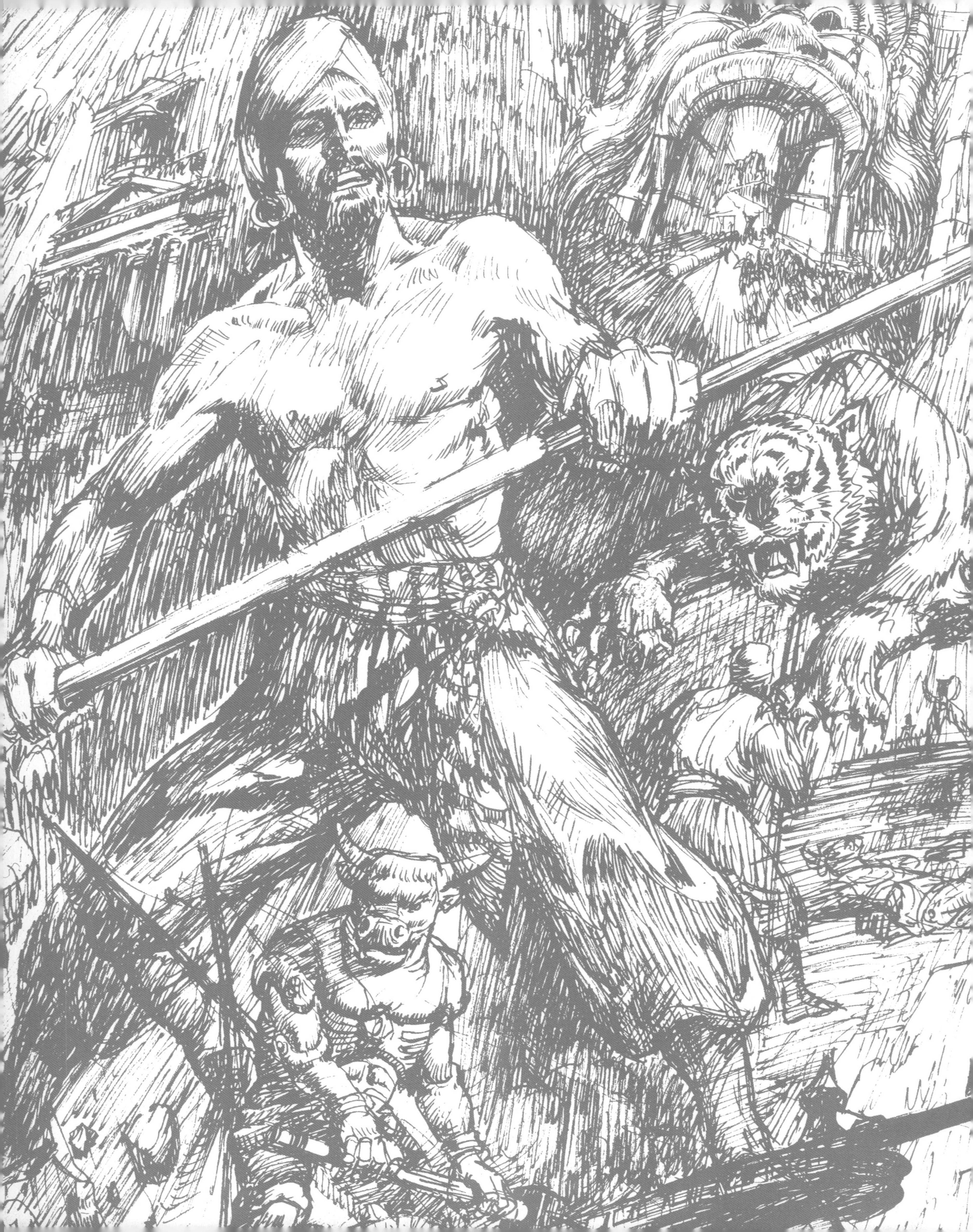

CHAPTER ELEVEN

THE GOLDEN VOYAGE OF SINBAD (1973)
SINBAD AND THE EYE OF THE TIGER (1977)

CO-PRODUCER AND SPECIAL VISUAL EFFECTS: RAY HARRYHAUSEN

THE GOLDEN VOYAGE OF SINBAD: Sinbad agrees to help the Grand Vizier of Marabia locate the missing piece of a golden amulet that will reveal a map to the fabled Fountain of Destiny. But the evil magician Prince Koura is determined to use the Fountain's gifts to conquer Marabia. Accompanied by the beautiful slave girl Margiana, Sinbad sets sail for the lost continent of Lemuria. En route he and his crew encounter a number of strange creatures brought to life by Koura's black magic, including a wooden siren figurehead, a six-armed statue of Kali, a one-eyed centaur and a bat-like creature called homunculus. After a battle between the centaur and the Fountain guardian, a giant griffin, Sinbad finally defeats Koura in a sword fight to the death.

SINBAD AND THE EYE OF THE TIGER: Sinbad arrives in the port of Charak to ask Prince Kassim for permission to marry his sister, Princess Farah. But the prince's evil stepmother Zenobia, determined to see her son rule the kingdom instead, has turned Kassim into a baboon. Sinbad vows to help undo the curse by seeking the alchemist Melanthius on the island of Casgar. Furious at Sinbad's involvement, Zenobia uses her magic powers to conjure up a trio of ghouls, and then pursues Sinbad with the assistance of a giant bronze monster called Minoton. Melanthius sends them to the ancient land of Hyperborea for the antidote and perils along the way include an attack by a giant walrus and a sabre-toothed tiger.

DYNARAMA MEANS ADVENTURE!
THE GOLDEN VOYAGE OF SINBAD

Shortly after the completion of *First Men in the Moon* (1964), Ray set to work on a number of key sketches that he felt would make a fine fantasy picture in the tradition of his previous films, such as *The 7th Voyage of Sinbad* and *Jason and the Argonauts*. This included images of a centaur battling with a gryphon and a multi-armed statue sword fighting with a group of men. Little did he realise it at the time, but these pictures were to be the genesis of *The Golden Voyage of Sinbad*, which became the next project after *The Valley of Gwangi*.

In 1971, Ray dusted off the pictures and presented them to Charles Schneer, along with a rough outline of a story he called *Sinbad's 8th Voyage*, combining the mythical characters and architecture of India and the Middle East. Schneer was captivated by the idea and assigned writer Brian Clemens (*Captain Kronos*) to turn Ray's ideas into a screenplay. Now called *Sinbad's Golden Voyage*, Ray, who was also the film's co-producer (a role he played on all his subsequent movies), had a clearer picture of which areas of the story would be suitable for Dynamation (renamed Dynarama on the publicity). Now there were characters like a sword-wielding statue called Kali, a tiny bat-like creature called a homunculus, and a living ship's figurehead to accompany his original concept of a cyclopean centaur and a winged gryphon.

THIS PAGE: Two examples of Ray's stunning pre-production art for the film (the arrival at Lemuria and the fight with Kali).

HARRYHAUSEN THE MOVIE POSTERS

The cast for the film included John Phillip Law (*Barbarella*) as the hero, Sinbad; Tom Baker (*Doctor Who*) as the evil magician, Prince Koura; Caroline Munro (*Captain Kronos*) as the beautiful heroine Margiana; Douglas Wilmer (*Jason and the Argonauts*) as the golden masked Vizier, and Martin Shaw (*The Professionals*) as a loyal member of Sinbad's crew, Rachid.

Gordon Hessler (*Cry of the Banshee*) was chosen to direct the movie, with Ted Moore (*A Man For All Seasons*) as the director of cinematography. Miklós Róza (*The Thief of Bagdad*) was commissioned to write the musical score.

Although hoping to make the film in India, production difficulties meant that Ray and Schneer once again took advantage of the evocative scenery of Spain to shoot all the live-action footage, even revisiting locations that had proved so useful in earlier films such as *The 7th Voyage of Sinbad*. Now Palma and Majorca were doubling for such exotic and romantic settings as the Temple of the Oracle of All Knowledge, the Fountain of Destiny and the fictional *Arabian Nights* land of Marabia. Interior sets for the film were constructed in Madrid's Verona Studios, including the scenes aboard Sinbad's ship. The mysterious island of Lemuria was fashioned from detailed miniatures and glass paintings segued with the live-action footage via blue screen traveling mattes.

During the eleven months that followed, Ray toiled away in his tiny workshop at London's Goldhawk Studios, filming the complex animation scenes. Dynarama highlights included the attack on Sinbad's ship by its Siren figurehead; the bronze statue Kali (in reality a twelve-inch-high model), who is brought magically to life by Koura and challenges Sinbad and his men to a fierce sword battle (a sequence almost as complex to choreograph and animate as the skeleton fight in *Jason and the Argonauts*), and the climactic battle between the centaur and the guardian of the Fountain of Destiny, a monster-sized gryphon.

The Golden Voyage of Sinbad cost just under one million dollars to make, and was a huge success at the box office, earning over twelve million dollars worldwide. It opened in the UK on December 20th, 1973 at London's Odeon Marble Arch. General release followed through December and into January 1974 on the Odeon cinema circuit accompanied by a children's drama called *Lost in the Desert*. Four months later it debuted in America on a double-bill with a western called *Santee*.

The film was also backed up by an elaborate advertizing campaign, with some stunning poster art, as well as tie-in merchandise that included comic books, a novelization and various items of apparel. The film was also re-released in the UK two years later, and premiered on the commercial television network in 1982.

In America, Mort Künstler's artwork featured the villainous centaur as its centerpiece. In the UK campaign, British artist Brian Bysouth opted for brashly colored images of the film's leading actors, surrounded by various action sequences, including the Vizier's golden mask, the death-dealing Kali, and Sinbad's ship, its rigging ripped asunder by a ferocious storm.

One or two unusual poster designs for the film came from Eastern Europe. Polish artist J. Neugebauer chose a silhouette of Sinbad against a yellow sky (*Podroòż Sindbada Do Zkotej Krainy*), while Czechoslovakian artist Olga Fischerová's minimalist poster art features Kali being operated on strings like a puppet (*Zlatá, Sindibadova Cesta*).

The renaming of Ray's stop-motion process from Dynamation to Dynarama was also given a great deal of publicity on the posters. 'Sinbad battles the creatures of legend in the Miracle of Dynarama!' and 'Dynarama means Supreme Adventure!' were just two of the bylines, while an alternative American one-sheet poster was also distributed with the words Dynarama Zodiac emblazoned above a pot-pourri of Ray's magnificent stop-motion characters.

THIS PAGE: (Left) The centaur carries slave girl Margiana back to its lair. (Above) Actress Caroline Munro played the beautiful Margiana. (Caroline is also one of the trustees of The Ray and Diana Harryhausen Foundation.)

CHPATER ELEVEN **THE GOLDEN VOYAGE OF SINBAD** 153

SINBAD BATTLES THE CREATURES OF LEGEND
in the miracle of
Dynarama
COLUMBIA PICTURES Presents
A CHARLES H. SCHNEER Production
The Golden Voyage of Sinbad
A new dimension in motion picture entertainment
FILMED IN Dynarama
starring
JOHN PHILLIP LAW
CAROLINE MUNRO · TOM BAKER · Screenplay by BRIAN CLEMENS
Music by MIKLOS ROZSA · Creator of Special Visual Effects RAY HARRYHAUSEN
Produced by CHARLES H. SCHNEER and RAY HARRYHAUSEN · Directed by GORDON HESSLER
COLUMBIA PICTURES/A DIVISION OF COLUMBIA PICTURES INDUSTRIES, INC. A B-P Associates Feature
G GENERAL AUDIENCES
ALL AGES ADMITTED
STYLE A
73/319
"GOLDEN VOYAGE OF SINBAD"

CHPATER ELEVEN **THE GOLDEN VOYAGE OF SINBAD**

il Viaggio fantastico di S

LA COLUMBIA PICTURES PRESENTA UNA PRODUZI

CON **JOHN PHILLIP LAW** CAROLINE MUNRO TOM BAKER SCENEGGIATURA DI BRIAN CLEMENS
IDEATORE DEGLI EFFETTI SPECIALI VISIVI **RAY HARRYHAUSEN** PRODOTTO DA CHARLES H. SCHNEER E RAY HARRYHAUSEN REGIA DI GORDON HESSLER

PREVIOUS SPREAD: PAGE 154 US One-sheet (69 x 104cm) Art by Mort Künstler. Courtesy of Ray Harryhausen Archive. PAGE 155 US teaser One-sheet (69 x 104cm) Art by Mort Künstler. Courtesy of Simon Greetham Archive.

THIS SPREAD: Italian (69 x 104cm) Art by Brian Bysmouth. Courtesy of Ray Harryhausen Archive.

NEXT SPREAD: PAGE 158 (Clockwise from top left) Czechoslovakian (27 x 40cm) Art by Olga Fischerová. East German (58 x 84cm) Art by Vonderwerk. Courtesy of Jens Holzheuer Archive. Portuguese (69 x 104cm) Art by Mort Künstler. Courtesy of Ray Harryhausen Archive. Polish (58 x 83cm) Art by Jacek Neugebaur. PAGE 159 Japanese B2 (51 x 76cm) Courtesy of Ray Harryhausen Archive.

CHPATER ELEVEN **THE GOLDEN VOYAGE OF SINBAD**

158 | HARRYHAUSEN THE MOVIE POSTERS

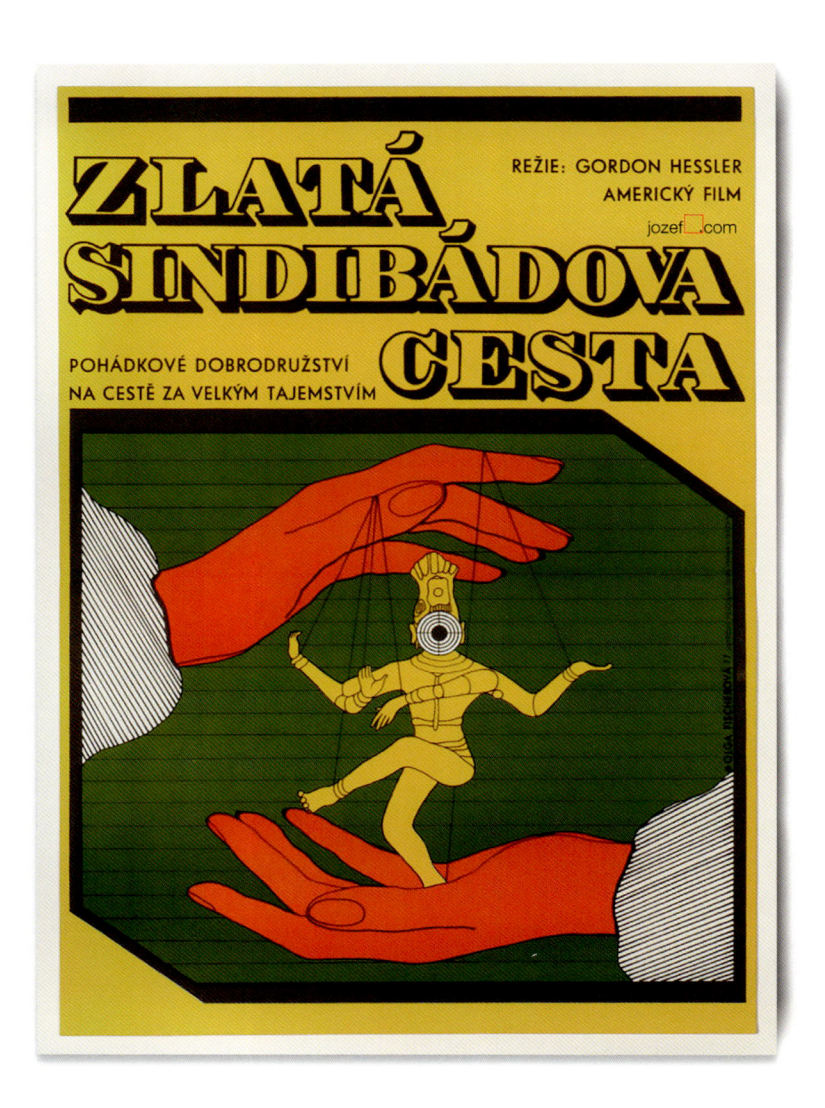

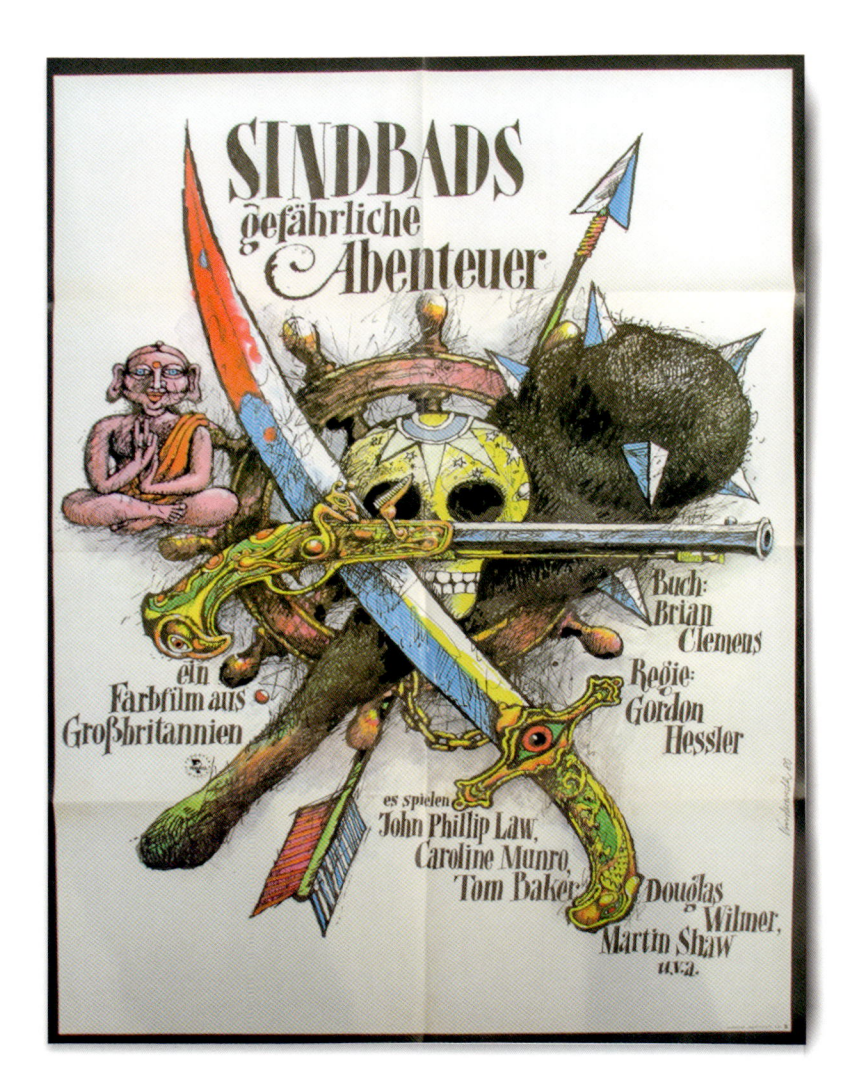

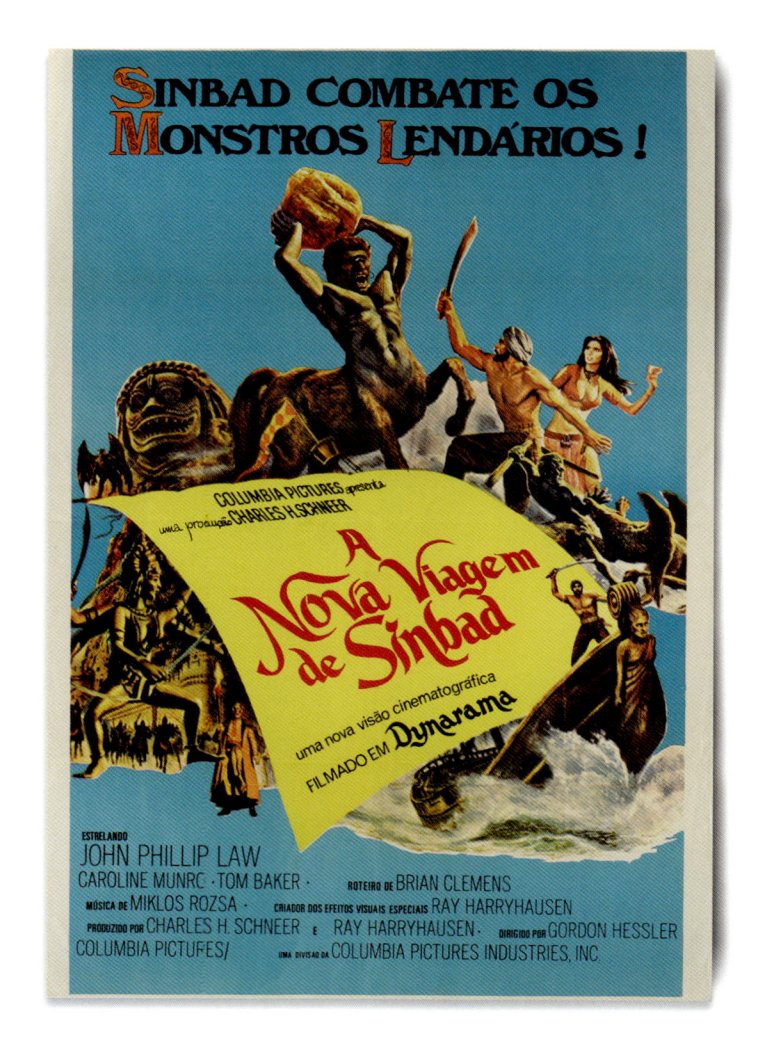

CHPATER ELEVEN **THE GOLDEN VOYAGE OF SINBAD**

SINBAD AND THE EYE OF THE TIGER

Although Ray had plenty of ideas that he could adapt into a new movie project, the box-office success of *The Golden Voyage of Sinbad* convinced both he and Schneer that another episode featuring the swashbuckling captain was in order. Ray immediately began developing an outline for a new story based on an idea he had originally considered using in the previous film: the premise of a prince being transformed into a monkey, possibly a baboon. By May 1974 Ray had also presented a number of drawings, details of characters and suggestions for location shooting to Schneer.

With Ray's story set in the mythical land of Hyperborea near the North Pole, Schneer asked writer Beverley Cross (*Jason and the Argonauts*) to flesh out a treatment. Columbia Pictures gave the go-ahead and by June 1975 work began on *Sinbad and the Eye of the Tiger*.

Casting for the film included Patrick Wayne (*The People That Time Forgot*) as Sinbad, newcomer Taryn Power as Dione, and Kurt Christian (*The Golden Voyage of Sinbad*) as Rafi, the evil son of the film's villainess Zenobia, played by veteran stage and screen actress Margaret Whiting. Additional cast members included Patrick Troughton (*Jason and the Argonauts*) as Melanthius and Jane Seymour (*Live and Let Die*) as the heroine, Princess Farah. With the actors in place, the role of director fell to former actor Sam Wanamaker, while Ted Moore (*The Golden Voyage of Sinbad*) was the director of photography. The film's score was composed by Roy Budd (*Get Carter*).

THIS PAGE: (Above) The sabre-tooth tiger of the film. (Below) Sinbad fights one of the ghouls — a difficult scene to animate as the stop-motion creature was armed with a flaming torch.

Locations included the Pyrenees and the mysterious ruins of Petra in Jordan, while areas of Spain once again provided backdrops for the film, including the city of Charak, the valley of Hyperborea, and Zenobia's palace. Live-action interiors and exteriors, including blue screen shots, were filmed in a disused RAF airfield hangar in Malta.

Ray spent thirteen months at Lee International Studios in west London completing all the Dynarama sequences and special effects. The ghouls scene, in which Sinbad fights three skeletal-like figures with bug eyes and exposed muscles that rise up from a camp fire, was particularly complex to animate due to the fact that one of the creatures brandishes a flaming torch.

Ray's *piece de resistance*, however, is the personality that he imbues into the character of the baboon. Because of the circumstances surrounding its existence in the story (a man magically transformed into a primate), Ray creates a sympathetic character with human traits and a performance that harks back to the emotion he skillfully gave the characters of Joe the gorilla in *Mighty Joe Young*, the Venusian Ymir in *20 Million Miles to Earth*, and the tiny homunculus in *The Golden Voyage of Sinbad*.

The Minaton, a giant mechanical slave of Zenobia with the torso of a man and the head of a bull, was one of Ray's more unusual creations. Its stiff robotic movements are more in keeping with the bronze statue Talos from *Jason and the Argonauts* or Bubo the clockwork owl in *Clash of the Titans*. Other marvelous creatures brought to life through the magic of Dynarama included a giant wasp, a monstrous walrus, and a club-wielding Troglodyte — a humanoid creature with a horned head that accompanies Sinbad and his men on their journey to Hyperborea.

At the climax of the film, the club-wielding Troglodyte and the Guardian of the Shrine of the Four Elements, a fearsome sabre-toothed tiger, are locked in mortal combat. A complex and detailed stop-motion sequence that took several months to film, it is one that conjures up similar confrontations in *The 7th Voyage of Sinbad* (Cyclops versus dragon) and *The Golden Voyage of Sinbad* (one-eyed centaur versus gryphon).

Sinbad and the Eye of the Tiger took a total of three years to complete, and opened in America in May 1977. It debuted in London on the 14th July at both the Columbia cinema in Shaftesbury Avenue and at the Odeon Kensington, with a general release through the Odeon cinema circuit from August on a double-bill with an adventure drama called *Lost in the Wild*. *Supersnooper* and *Spider-Man* were also supporting features according to some of the UK double-bill quad posters.

Columbia spent a vast amount on publicity and produced some stunning art for both the American and UK releases. One eye-catching design by artist Victor Gadino features an action pose of Sinbad, while another makes the villain Zenobia's character more prominent. The latter painting, showing a taloned foot reaching out from beneath Zenobia's cloak by artist Birney Lettick (1919-1986), was used by most of the overseas distributors. One exception was artist Disman's surreal artwork for the Czechoslovakian release: rolling black waves against a mauve sun!

Considering that there's a scene in the film in which Seymour and Power show more flesh than was usual for a Ray Harryhausen production (with the obvious exception of *One Million Years B.C.*) it's amazing that Columbia didn't incorporate this into its poster campaign.

Costing three times as much as *The Golden Voyage of Sinbad* (nearer seven million dollars) the cost of production was unfortunately not reflected in the box office receipts. While it was successful worldwide, it couldn't capture the novelty value of the previous film. *Sinbad and the Eye of the Tiger* was, however, listed among the Rank Organisation's top-ten box-office attractions for the year and finally made its UK commercial television debut in 1988.

THIS PAGE: (Left) The cover for the promotional handbook of the film. (Above) Advance artwork for the film's publicity by an unkown artist.

CHPATER ELEVEN **SINBAD AND THE EYE OF THE TIGER**

HARRYHAUSEN THE MOVIE POSTERS

THIS SPREAD: (Far Left) US Teaser One-sheet (69 x 104cm) Art by Birney Lettick. Courtesy of Ray Harryhausen Archive. (Above) British Quad (76 x 102cm) Art by Victor Gadino. Courtesy of Simon Greetham Archive. (Left) German (58 x 84cm) Art by Birney Lettick. Courtesy of Ray Harryhausen Archive.

CHPATER ELEVEN **SINBAD AND THE EYE OF THE TIGER**

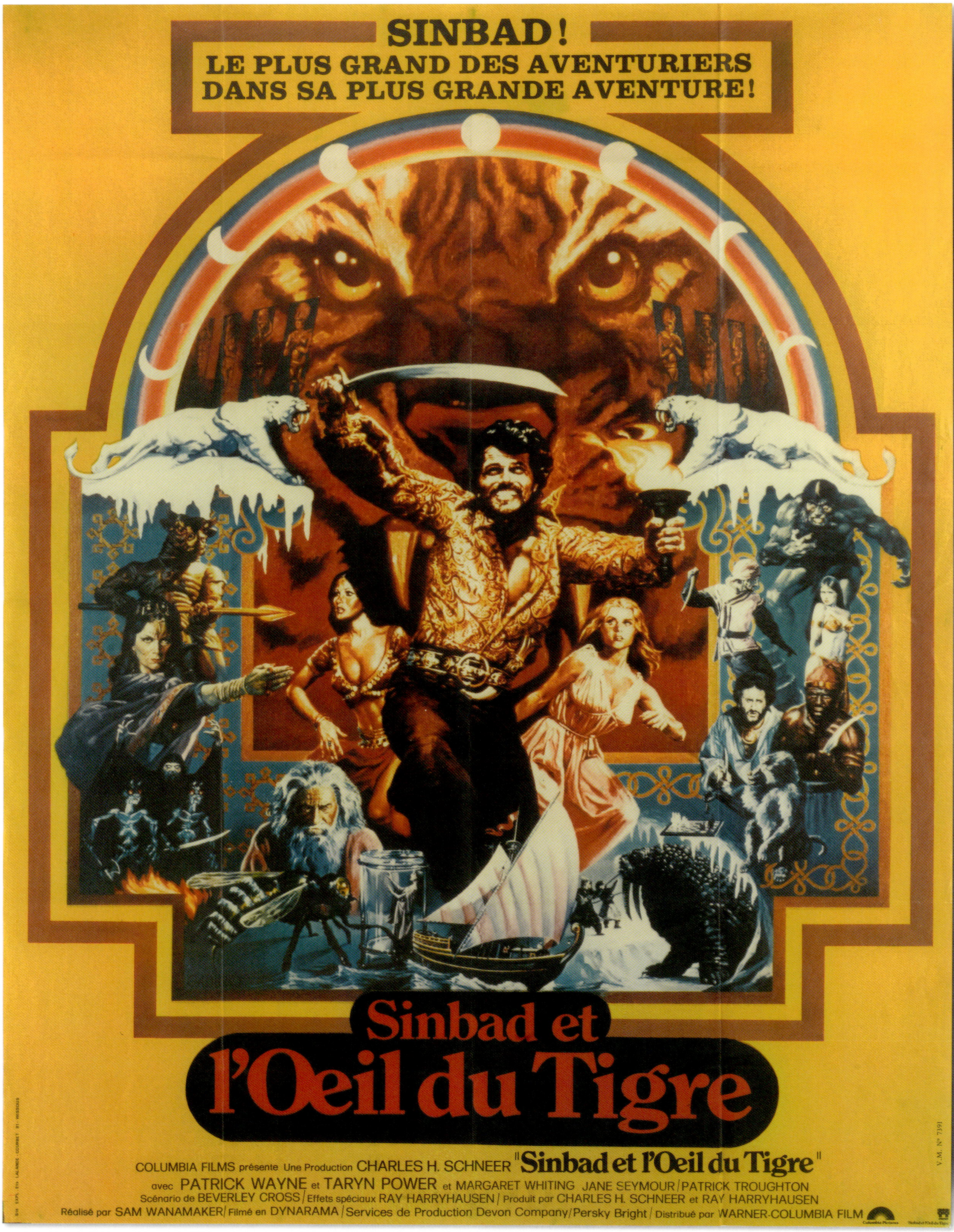
SINBAD!
LE PLUS GRAND DES AVENTURIERS
DANS SA PLUS GRANDE AVENTURE!
Sinbad et
l'Oeil du Tigre
COLUMBIA FILMS présente Une Production CHARLES H. SCHNEER "Sinbad et l'Oeil du Tigre"
avec PATRICK WAYNE et TARYN POWER et MARGARET WHITING JANE SEYMOUR/PATRICK TROUGHTON
Scénario de BEVERLEY CROSS/Effets spéciaux RAY HARRYHAUSEN/ Produit par CHARLES H. SCHNEER et RAY HARRYHAUSEN
Réalisé par SAM WANAMAKER/ Filmé en DYNARAMA/Services de Production Devon Company/Persky Bright/ Distribué par WARNER-COLUMBIA FILM
V.M. N° 7391

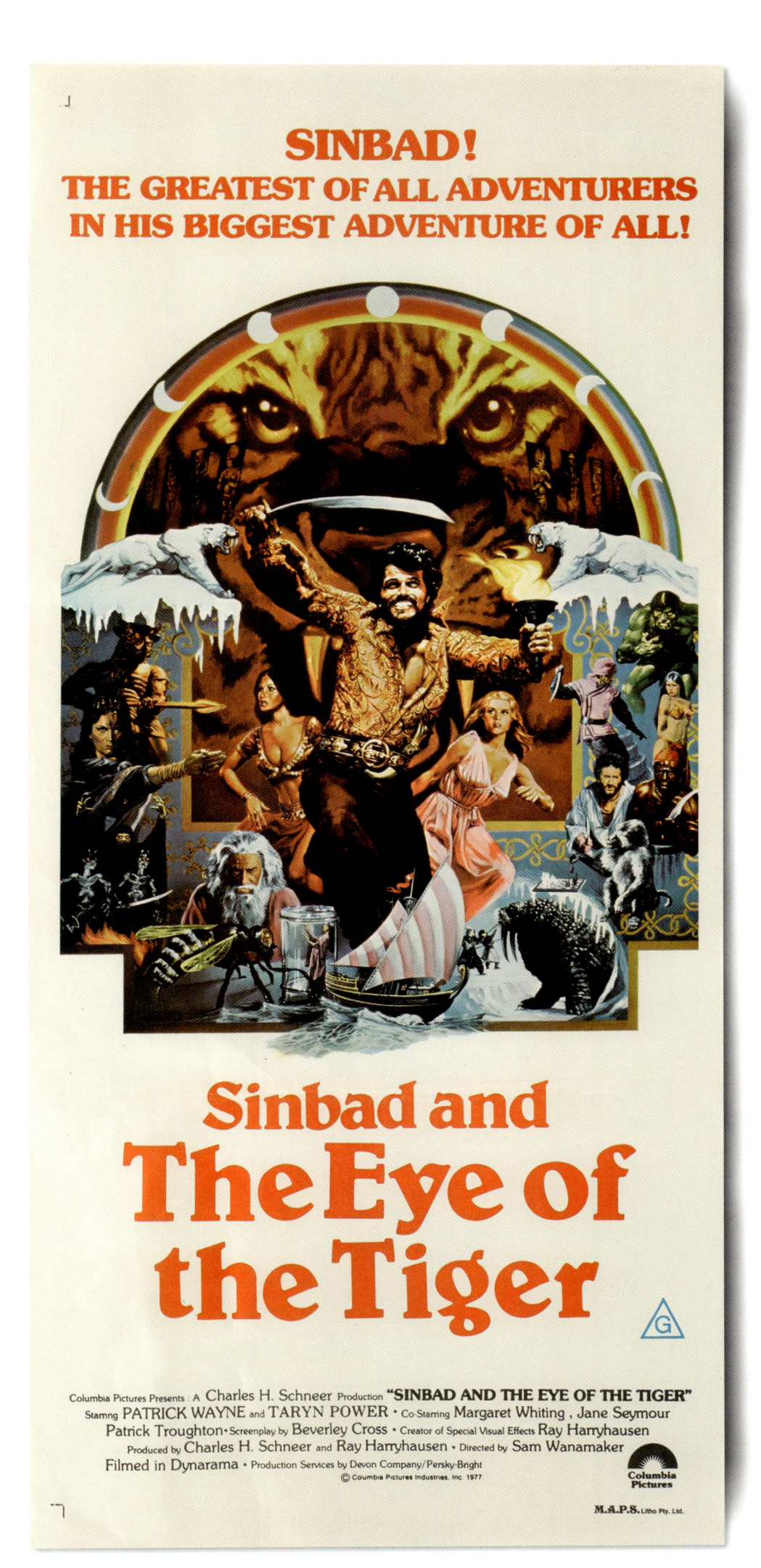

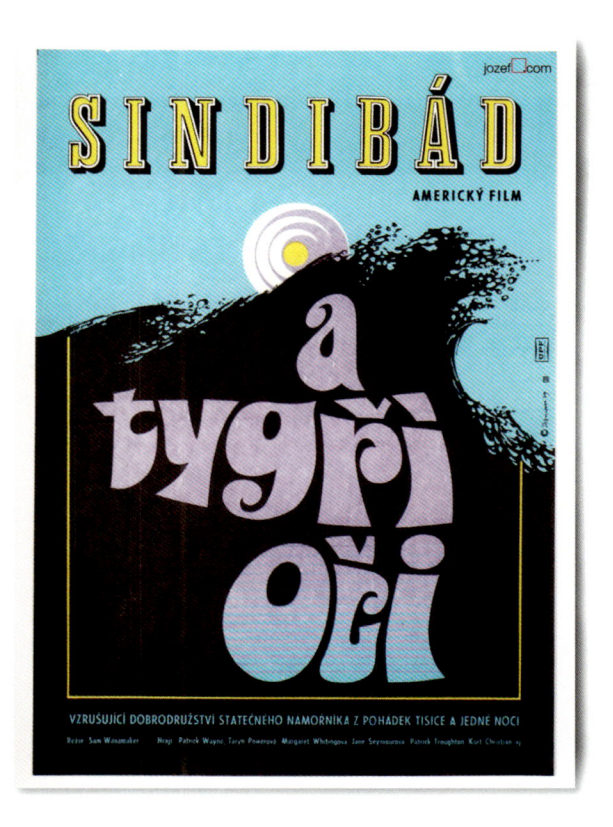

THIS SPREAD: (Opposite) French Grande (115 x 157cm) Art by Birney Lettick. Courtesy of Ray Harryhausen Archive. (Left) Australian Daybill (34 x 77cm) Art by Birney Lettick. Courtesy of Ray Harryhausen Archive. (Top Right) Czechoslovakian (29 x 42cm) Art by Miloslav Disman. (Bottom Right) Japanese B2 (51 x76cm) Art by Birney Lettick. Courtesy of Ray Harryhausen Archive.

CHPATER ELEVEN **SINBAD AND THE EYE OF THE TIGER** 165

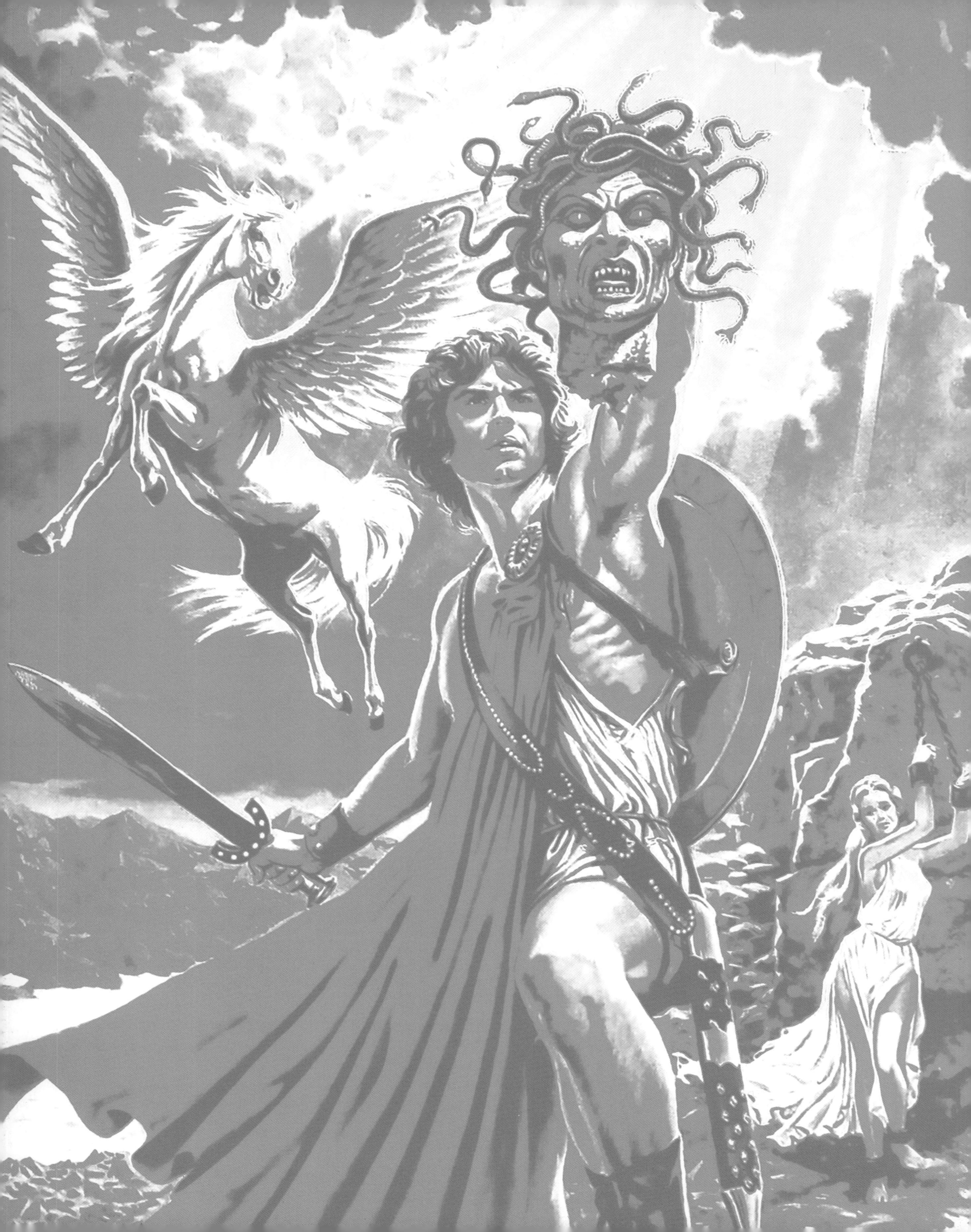

CHAPTER TWELVE

CLASH OF THE TITANS (1981)

CO-PRODUCER AND SPECIAL VISUAL EFFECTS: RAY HARRYHAUSEN

Perseus and his mother escape from the city of Argos before it's completely destroyed by one of the last of the Titans, a gigantic sea beast called the Kraken. Called upon by the Gods of Mount Olympus to free the Princess Andromeda from the evil half-man, half-monster Calibos, Perseus is helped in his task by an elderly playwright called Ammon. But the journey is fraught with danger, including an attack by giant scorpions, a ferocious battle with a two-headed dog called Dioskilos and an encounter with the evil Medusa, whose eyes can turn any living thing to stone. Having defeated Calibos, Perseus must then rescue Andromeda from the Kraken. As the monstrous Titan rises from the sea to claim its prize, Perseus comes to the rescue on the winged horse Pegasus.

AN ENTERTAINMENT SPECTACULAR!

With the release of *Star Wars* in 1977 and *Close Encounters of the Third Kind* in 1978, Hollywood was clamouring to cash in on the phenomenon with space adventures of its own. But Ray wasn't keen on the idea of jumping on the science fiction bandwagon, preferring instead to stick with the world of myths and legends for his next film.

For a long time he had been considering the story of Perseus and the Gorgon as an ideal subject matter for Dynarama. By a curious coincidence, scriptwriter Beverley Cross had also been working on a similar concept.

When Columbia Pictures, who had enjoyed financial success with Ray's previous Sinbad films, rejected the Perseus story as being too costly, Schneer made a deal with MGM, who not only liked the idea, but were prepared to lavish a great deal of money (16 million dollars) on the project.

With a lot of money to throw at the acting talent (although not necessarily the special effects budget), the studio secured leading stage and screen actor Laurence Olivier (*Henry V*) in the role of Zeus, Maggie Smith (*Harry Potter and the Order of the Phoenix*) as Thetis, Claire Bloom (*The Haunting*) as Hera, Ursula Andress (*Dr. No*) as Aphrodite, Flora Robson (*The Sea Hawk*) as one of the three Stygian Witches and Burgess Meredith (*Rocky*) as the playwright Ammon.

Newcomers Harry Hamlin (*Movie Movie*) and Judi Bowker (*Brother Sun, Sister Moon*) were chosen to play the hero Perseus and the damsel-in-distress Andromeda respectively. Desmond Davis (*Smashing Time*) was chosen to direct the film, now called *Clash of the Titans*, and the film's rousing musical score was written by Laurence Rosenthal (*Meteor*).

THIS PAGE: (Above) Perseus battles with the giant scorpions. (Top Left) Harry Hamlin as Perseus, with Judi Bowker as Andromeda. (Bottom Left) Filming the destruction of the City of Argos by tidal wave.

Spain, Malta and Italy provided the diverse locations needed for the film, including the untapped beauty of Guadix, the mountains of Antequera, the beaches at Palinuro, the temples at Paestum (previously used for the Harpies sequence in *Jason and the Argonauts*) and the rocky terrain on the island of Gozo. All the film's interiors were shot either inside the aircraft hangar in Malta (where sections of *Sinbad and the Eye of the Tiger* had been filmed), or at Pinewood Studios.

To make the story of Perseus and his confrontation with the snake-haired Gorgon, Medusa, more exciting, Ray added other mythological creatures to the mix, some of whom were already associated with the legend, including the flying horse Pegasus. Among the stop-motion supporting players were the hideously deformed and sadistic Calibos, a two-headed dog called Dioskilos, and the multi-armed Kraken. Additional screen time was given to three giant scorpions, a colossal vulture, and a tiny clockwork owl called Bubo.

But with so many characters to animate, Ray broke a habit of a lifetime and employed two assistant animators, Steven Archer (*Krull*) and industry veteran Jim Danforth (*When Dinosaurs Ruled the Earth*), to help cut the workload and keep the film on schedule. Even so, Ray still spent eighteen months on the Dynarama scenes (though the name wasn't referred to on any of the film's publicity).

Aside from animating the many adversaries that Perseus has to face in his quest to kill Medusa and rescue Andromeda from the clutches of the Kraken, Ray also supervised the destruction by earthquake and tsunami of the city of Argos (actually an intricately detailed five-foot-high miniature), the mountainous home of the gods (Mount Olympus), and all the necessary blue-screen photography that seamlessly blended together both the actors and the stop-motion creatures.

Although the performance of the skyscraper-high Kraken rising from the ocean floor to kill Andromeda is a fine example of Ray's skills as an animator, it is the confrontation between Perseus and the bare-breasted Medusa that is the most impressive sequence in the film. Avoiding the Gorgon's deadly stare, which turns people to stone, the young hero slays the vile monster against a backdrop of twisted columns and flickering torchlight. Perseus and his fight with Medusa remains to this day a masterpiece of special effects cinema, and a lasting tribute to Ray and his work.

Clash of the Titans opened in America in June 1981, with one critic referring to it as 'Ray's *Gone With the Wind*'. The UK release followed at the Empire Leicester Square on July 2nd, followed by general release on the Odeon cinema circuit from July 26th. It was slightly cut by the censor in the UK to secure an A certificate and went on to gross over 70 million dollars worldwide, finally making its UK television debut on the BBC in 1986. At the time of release, the film was also heavily merchandised with a wide assortment of tie-in books and comics. It was also the first of Ray's movies to spawn a series of action figures.

MGM launched an elaborate campaign to promote the film with a range of different poster artwork. Perseus cleaving the screen in two with his sword by American artist Roger Huyssen proved a popular choice on both the German (*Kampf Der Titanen*) and UK posters (the latter blatantly including a tie-in competition with Smiths Snacks).

The American advance one-sheet featured artist S. Gorga's striking image of the Kraken rising from the sea before a terrified Andromeda, with the stars of the film pictured down the right-hand side. A stunning design by Greg and Tim Hildebrant, who painted the teaser posters for the *Star Wars* (1977) promotion, includes Medusa and an interpretation of the film's main stars standing next to Pegasus (Hamlin and Bowker had yet to be cast in the roles).

Some of the most striking artwork appeared on the Italian poster (*Scontro Di Titani*) by Bruno Napoli, showing Perseus holding up the severed head of the Gorgon, Pegasus circling in the sky above him, and Andromeda shackled to the rocks in the background. The Belgian and French posters (*Le Choc Des Titans*), by artist Jean Mascii (1926–2003), opted for a similar pose with Perseus and the Gorgon's head, flanked by scenes from the film including Zeus and the gods of Mount Olympus. In East Germany, the anonymous artist hired to illustrate the film poster chose a large image of the Gorgon, while the Indian and Japanese distributors produced posters with a montage of the American artwork.

> The confrontation between Perseus and the bare-breasted Medusa is the most impressive sequence in the film.

THIS PAGE: (Left) Harry Hamlin and Judi Bowker. (Above) Perseus with Medusa's head.

CHPATER TWELVE **CLASH OF THE TITANS**

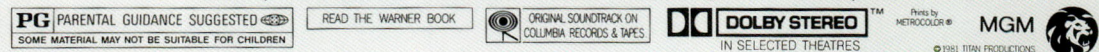

HARRYHAUSEN THE MOVIE POSTERS

CHPATER TWELVE **CLASH OF THE TITANS**

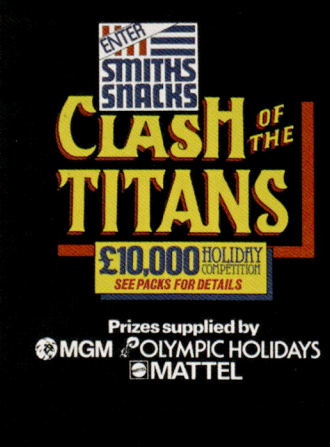

HARRYHAUSEN THE MOVIE POSTERS

Metro-Goldwyn-Mayer Presents
À CHARLES H. SCHNEER Production
"CLASH OF THE TITANS"
Starring HARRY HAMLIN as Perseus
JUDI BOWKER as Andromeda
BURGESS MEREDITH
MAGGIE SMITH
URSULA ANDRESS
CLAIRE BLOOM · SIAN PHILLIPS
FLORA ROBSON
and LAURENCE OLIVIER as Zeus
Creator of Special Visual Effects
RAY HARRYHAUSEN
Music by LAURENCE ROSENTHAL
Written by BEVERLEY CROSS
Produced by CHARLES H. SCHNEER and
RAY HARRYHAUSEN
Directed by DESMOND DAVIS
READ THE FUTURA PAPERBACK
ORIGINAL SOUNDTRACK AVAILABLE
ON CBS RECORDS & TAPES   PRINTS BY METROCOLOR®
DISTRIBUTED BY CINEMA INTERNATIONAL CORPORATION
MGM COPYRIGHT© 1981 TITAN PRODUCTIONS
DOLBY STEREO
IN SELECTED THEATRES

PRINTED IN ENGLAND BY W. E. BERRY LTD. BRADFORD

PREVIOUS SPREAD: PAGE 170 US One-sheet Teaser (69 x 104cm) Art by Greg and Tim Hildebrandt. PAGE 171 US One-sheet Teaser (69 x 104cm) Art by Daniel Goozee.

THIS SPREAD: (Left) British Quad (76 x 102cm) Art by Roger Huyssen. Courtesy of Simon Greetham Archive. (Above) Belgian (36 x 48cm) Courtesy of Mike Hankin Archive.

NEXT SPREAD: PAGE 174 Swedish (69 x 104cm) Courtesy of Ray Harryhausen Archive. PAGE 175 German A1 (58 x 84cm) Art by Roger Huyssen. Courtesy of Ray Harryhausen Archive.

CHPATER TWELVE **CLASH OF THE TITANS** 173

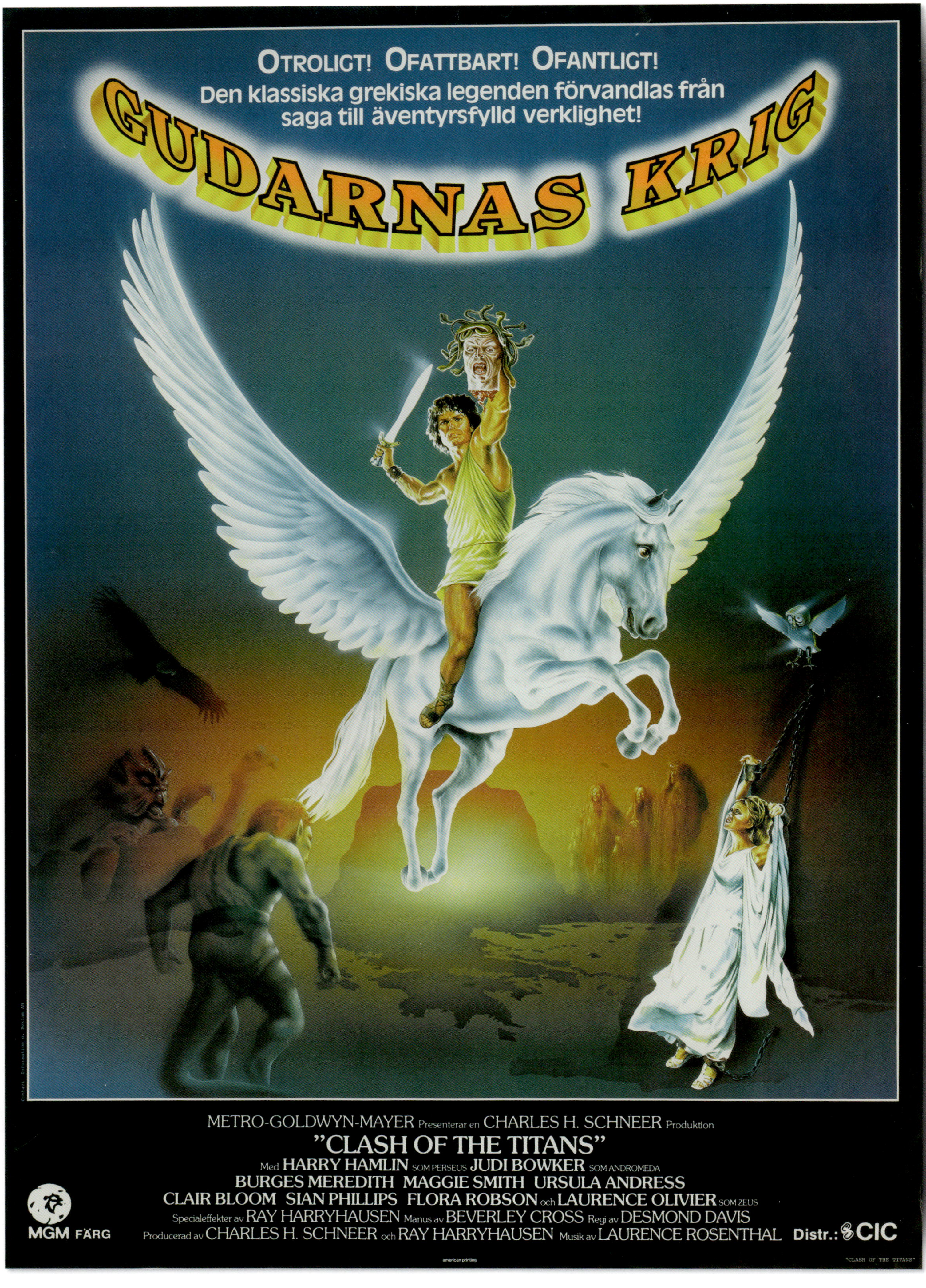
OTROLIGT! OFATTBART! OFANTLIGT!
Den klassiska grekiska legenden förvandlas från saga till äventyrsfylld verklighet!
GUDARNAS KRIG
METRO-GOLDWYN-MAYER Presenterar en CHARLES H. SCHNEER Produktion
"CLASH OF THE TITANS"
Med HARRY HAMLIN SOM PERSEUS JUDI BOWKER SOM ANDROMEDA
BURGES MEREDITH MAGGIE SMITH URSULA ANDRESS
CLAIR BLOOM SIAN PHILLIPS FLORA ROBSON och LAURENCE OLIVIER SOM ZEUS
Specialeffekter av RAY HARRYHAUSEN Manus av BEVERLEY CROSS Regi av DESMOND DAVIS
Producerad av CHARLES H. SCHNEER och RAY HARRYHAUSEN Musik av LAURENCE ROSENTHAL
MGM FÄRG
Distr.: CIC
american printing
"CLASH OF THE TITANS"

CHPATER TWELVE **CLASH OF THE TITANS**

HARRYHAUSEN THE MOVIE POSTERS

CHPATER TWELVE **CLASH OF THE TITANS**

KAMPF DER TITANEN
Ein Farbfilm aus den USA mit Laurence Olivier, Burgess Meredith, Harry Hamlin, Judi Bowker u. v. a.
Regie: Desmond Davis
Progress Film-Verleih

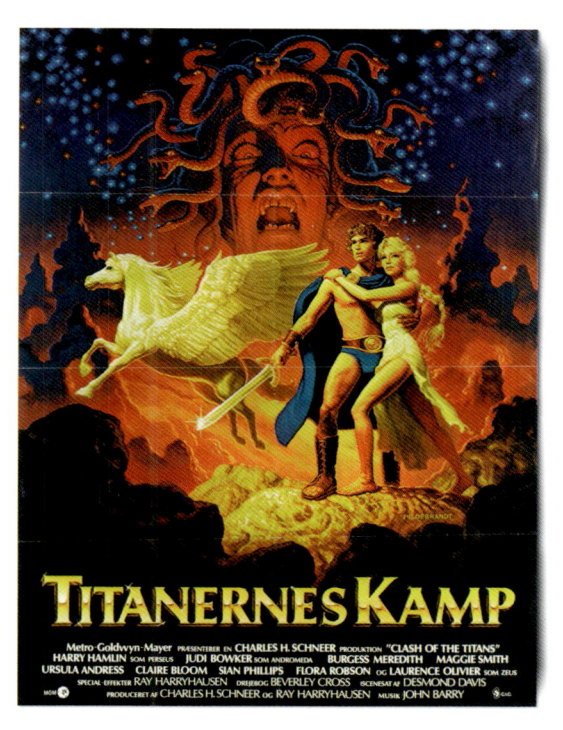

PREVIOUS SPREAD: PAGE 176 Thailand (69 x 104cm) Courtesy of Ray Harryhausen Archive. PAGE 177 Italian 2 Fogli (99 x 140cm) Art by Bruno Napoli.

THIS SPREAD: (Opposite) East German (58 x 84cm) Courtesy of Ingo Strecker Archive. (Left) German A2 (40 x 58cm) Courtesy of Ray Harryhausen Archive. (Above) Danish (69 x 104cm) Courtesy of Ray Harryhausen Archive.

NEXT SPREAD: PAGE 180 Japanese B2 (51 x 76cm) Courtesy of Ray Harryhausen Archive. PAGE 181 Japanese B2 (51 x 76cm) Courtesy of Ray Harryhausen Archive.

CHPATER TWELVE **CLASH OF THE TITANS** 179

HARRYHAUSEN THE MOVIE POSTERS

CHPATER TWELVE **CLASH OF THE TITANS**

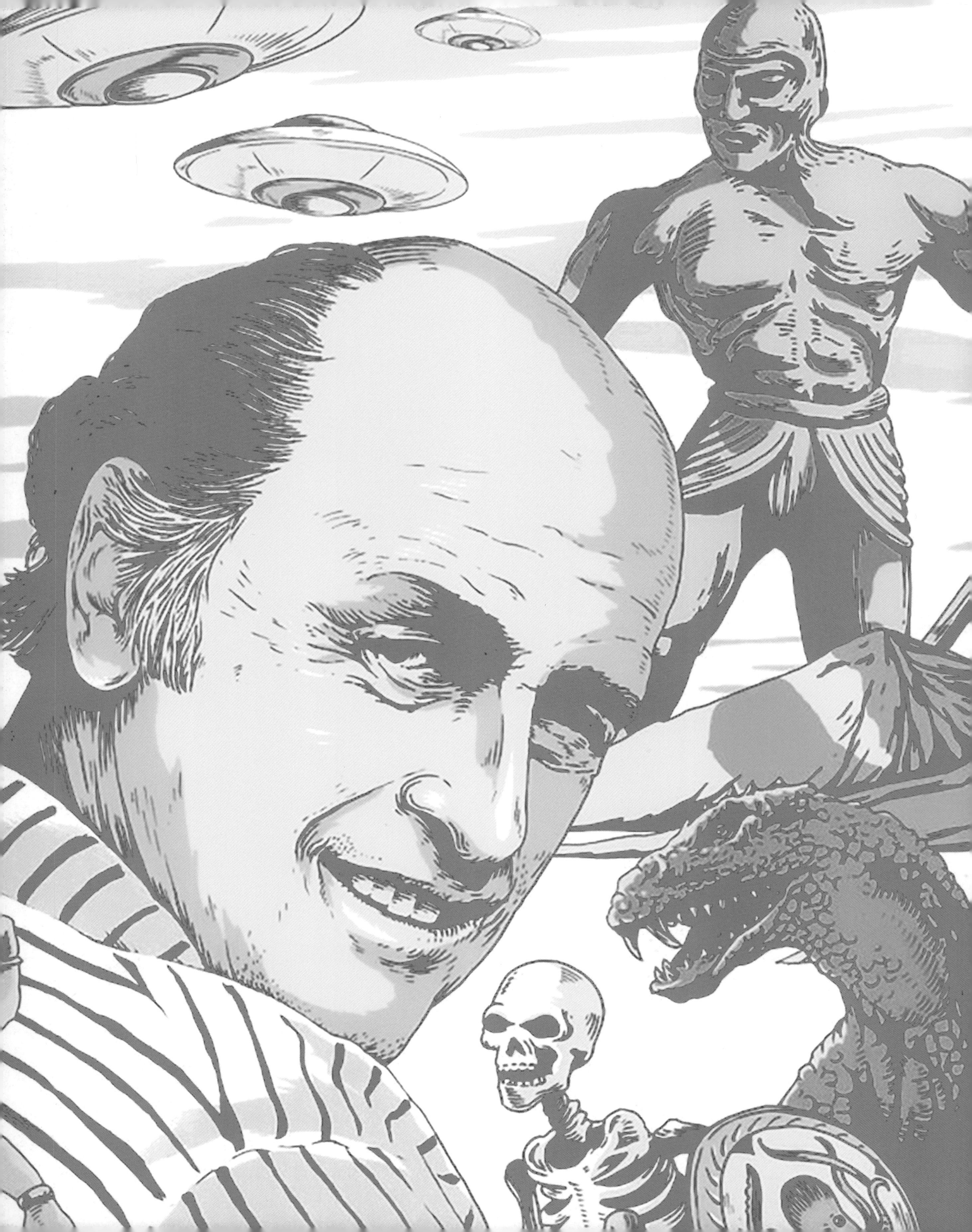

CHAPTER THIRTEEN

RAY HARRYHAUSEN: SPECIAL EFFECTS TITAN (2011)

THE LEGEND CONTINUES

After the completion of *Clash of the Titans* Ray worked on some preliminary sketches for a new film called *Force of the Trojans*. Written by Beverley Cross, the script was loosely based on Virgil's *Aeneid*, but while some considerable time was spent developing the project, it was canceled due to a lack of financial commitment from MGM.

Major studios were wary of the cost of stop-motion animation, particularly since the arrival of a new technology called CGI (Computer Generated Graphics) had taken the special effects industry by storm. Filmmakers were using computers to create a range of visual effects that a few years earlier would have been impossible. Films such as Ray's and the bespoke creatures that he had painstakingly constructed from materials like latex and cotton could now be designed and animated using computer software.

Ray was certainly impressed by the strides made in the art of special effects cinematography, but he was also the first to admit that the new technology wasn't for him. After decades of working in the time-consuming field of three-dimensional stop-motion animation his enthusiasm for making more films was waning. Without fully realizing it at the time, *Clash of the Titans* was to be his swansong, yet it was by no means the end of the story. His earlier films were more popular than ever thanks to numerous television screenings, video, DVD and Blu-ray releases.

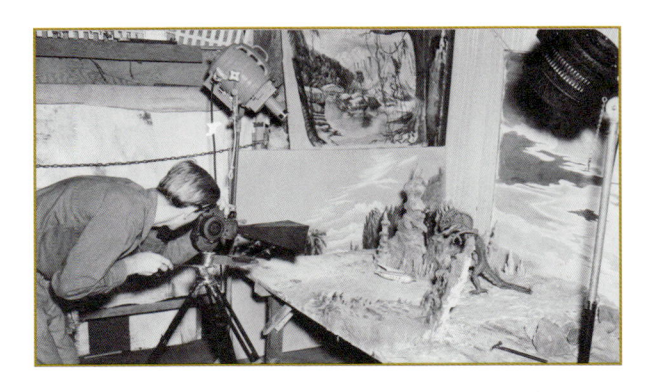

THIS SPREAD: (Above) Ray lines up a test shot for a never completed science fiction film featuring a creature called a Jupiterian. (Below) Ray poses with some of the characters he designed for *The Mother Goose Stories*. (Opposite) Ray with the stop-motion model of a ceratosaurus from *The Animal World*.

HARRYHAUSEN THE MOVIE POSTERS

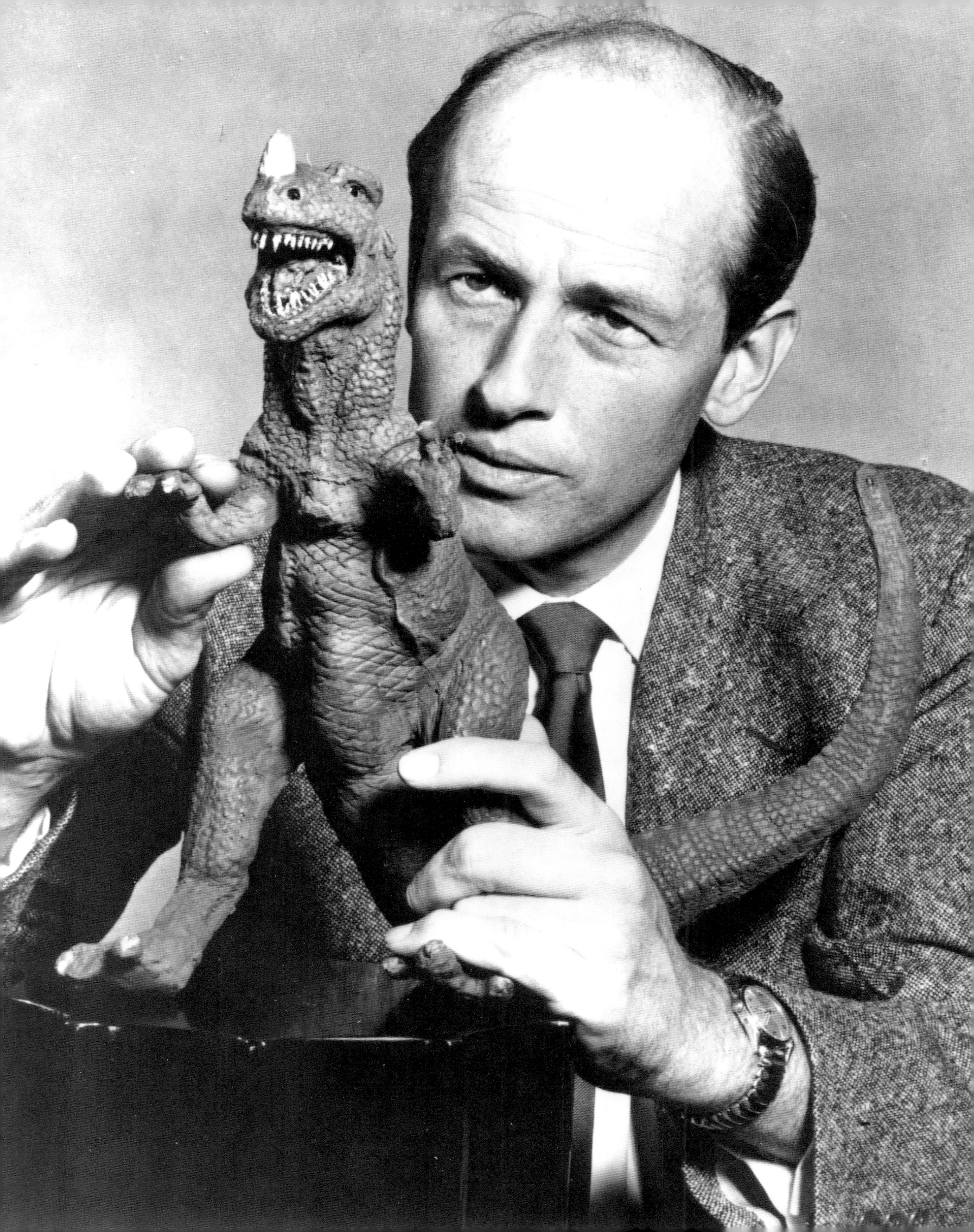

THIS PAGE: (Left) Ray animating the stop-motion figure of Mighty Joe Young. (Top Right) Ray demonstrates how to be picked up by a giant crab on the set of the film *Mysterious Island*. (Bottom Right) Dynarama in action! Ray lines up the stop-motion model of the Minaton to match the rear projected live-action footage (*Sinbad and the Eye of the Tiger*).

In fact, interest in Ray's work was gathering momentum around the world, with filmmakers like George Lucas and Steven Spielberg revealing in interviews how much of an influence his films had been in shaping their own careers. Leading visual effects animators working for companies such as Industrial Light and Magic and Digital Domain were looking to Ray's films for inspiration in creating their own special effects. And while the technology may have seemed light years ahead of Ray's Dynamation process, filmmakers were eager to share their secrets with the master of stop-motion animation. From *Jurassic Park* to *The Lord of the Rings*, Ray was a regular visitor to the sets, during both the shooting and post-production.

Accompanied by his wife Diana, Ray was busier than ever, accepting invitations to seminars, conventions and film festivals. Examples of his artwork and his highly detailed stop-motion models were exhibited throughout Europe and America. He was the subject of numerous interviews on both television and radio, while hundreds of column inches were written about him in magazines, newspapers and books.

It therefore came as no surprise in 2012 when French filmmakers Gilles Penso and Alexandre Poncet (*Creature Designers – The Frankenstein Complex*) released a documentary called *Ray Harryhausen: Special Effects Titan*. Featuring behind-the-scenes footage, interviews and film clips, the movie also boasted a roster of film industry guest stars, including directors and producers such as Peter Jackson (*The Lord of the Rings*), Terry Gilliam (*Brazil*), Guillermo del Toro (*Hellboy*), James Cameron (*Avatar*), Tim Burton (*Mars Attacks!*), John Landis (*An American Werewolf in London*), Nick Park (*Wallace and Gromit*), Steven Spielberg (*Jurassic Park*), Joe Dante (*Gremlins*) and John Lassiter (*Toy Story*). Science fiction author Ray Bradbury, visual effects supervisors Dennis Muren and Randy Cook, actress and friend Caroline Munro, and Ray's daughter Vanessa were also invited to take part.

For Penso and Poncet, who had seen some of Ray's *Mother Goose* animated fairy stories at school, and who compared Ray's pioneering achievements in special effects with those of French filmmaker George Méliès, the project was a labor of love. Penso, who wrote the script and composed an original music score for the film, spent eight years bringing the project to fruition. Extensive research into the subject

HARRYHAUSEN THE MOVIE POSTERS

resulted in a narrative that concentrated on the diversity of the films themselves, the inspiration behind them, the special effects work and their place in the fantasy genre. Knowing how much the name of Harryhausen was revered throughout the visual effects industry, Penso realized how important it was to include sound bites from some of the leading names in the field.

With an opening credits sequence that runs through a long list of contemporary fantasy movies from *Star Wars* to *The Lord of the Rings*, Penso's aim was to engage a younger audience, familiar with the latest science fiction and fantasy movies, but less knowledgeable about the making of films such as *Jason and the Argonauts* or *Clash of the Titans*.

Meeting up with Ray on several occasions to discuss the film, Penso and Poncet were given exclusive access to the archive of the Ray and Diana Harryhausen Foundation, a charitable trust set up in 1986 to preserve his legacy for future generations. 8mm home movies of Ray's early life and work, which were uncovered by his daughter Vanessa and special effects technician Randy Cook during a search of Ray's Los Angeles home, resulted in never-before-seen test footage of the arrival in New York of the *Beast from 20,000 Fathoms*, the alien spaceships hovering over the cities of the world in *Earth Vs. the Flying Saucers*, and the Ymir crashing through the walls of the Colosseum from *20 Million Miles to Earth*. Some rare color footage also came to light that showed the filming of the beach scenes on the Isle of Colossa in *The 7th Voyage of Sinbad*.

As Penso later opined, having access to these personal films was particularly fortuitous, as clearing film extracts from some of Ray's earlier films and those of other directors wasn't easy. But thanks to the involvement of film industry heavyweights like James Cameron and George Lucas, who were able to bring their considerable weight to bear in securing film clips from reluctant copyright holders, Penso and Poncet were able to make comparisons between Ray's films and scenes from both *Avatar* and *Star Wars*. The filmmakers also demonstrated how extensive study into the movement and positioning of Ray's dinosaurs in films such as *One Million Years B.C.* and *The Valley of Gwangi* proved to be an invaluable aid to the computer programmers responsible for animating the prehistoric creatures in the *Jurassic Park* franchise.

After an advance screening on November 27th 2011 at the Paris International Fantastic Film Festival, *Ray Harryhausen: Special Effects Titan* received a UK premiere on November 9th, 2012 at the Gate Cinema in London, with Ray as the guest of honor. During a limited cinema release through Arrow Films, it was given a warm reception by the press, and then spent several months touring various film festivals around the world from Belgium to Mexico.

The stunning limited-edition quad poster, illustrated by artist Joe Wilson, proved to be a great talking point among fans. Wilson, who specializes in artwork that combines pencil, ink and digital color, captures the very essence of Ray's work, with a visual roll call of his most popular creatures, from *The Beast From 20,000 Fathoms* to *Clash of the Titans*.

The interest that the film *Ray Harryhausen: Special Effects Titan* generated in the media was immense. And Ray's remarkable achievements in the art of visual effects were still making the headlines when the sad news came on May 7th 2013 that the master animator, filmmaker, auteur, and special effects legend had passed away at the age of 92.

> *Clash of the Titans* was to be Ray's swansong, yet it was by no means the end of his story.

Fortunately, Ray Harryhausen has left behind an incredible legacy of cinematic excellence, and a portfolio of some of the greatest fantasy films ever made. From humble beginnings in the late 1940s, with his first full-length feature film *Mighty Joe Young*, to the star-studded mythological blockbuster *Clash of the Titans* in 1981, his impressive body of work has not only transcended criticism, it has fired the imagination of audiences the world over. Considered classics of the fantasy genre, his films will continue to inspire whole new generations of fans for many years to come.

THIS PAGE: (Left) Ray and his life-long business partner, producer Charles H. Schneer (*Sinbad and the Eye of the Tiger*). (Above) Ray celebrating his 90th Birthday with his wife Diana and his daughter Vanessa.

NEXT SPREAD: Ray admiring artist Joe Wilson's stunning quad poster for the 2011 documentary, *Ray Harryhausen: Special Effects Titan*.

CHPATER THIRTEEN **RAY HARRYHAUSEN: SPECIAL EFFECTS TITAN**

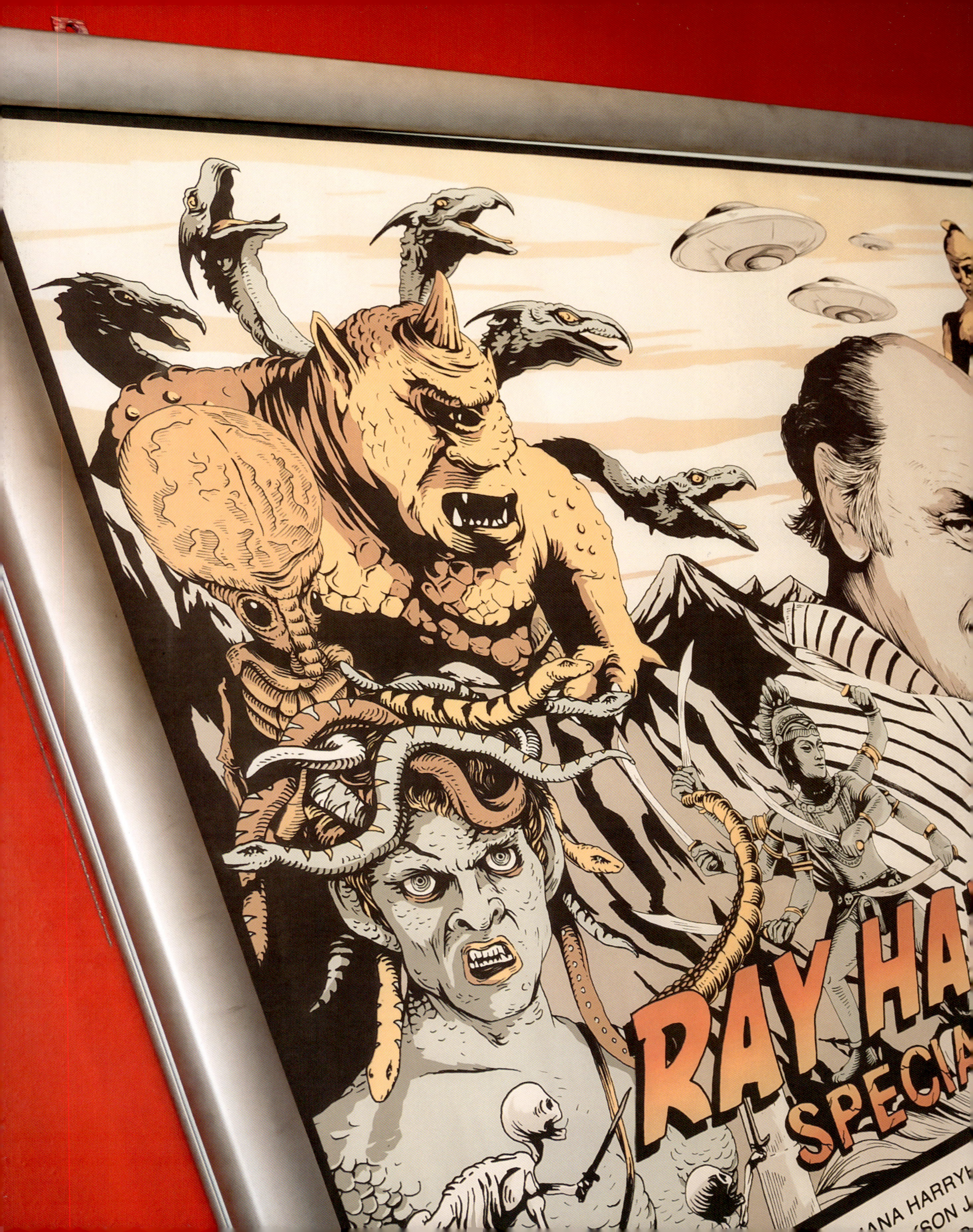
RAY HA
SPECIA
ANA HARRYH
SON J

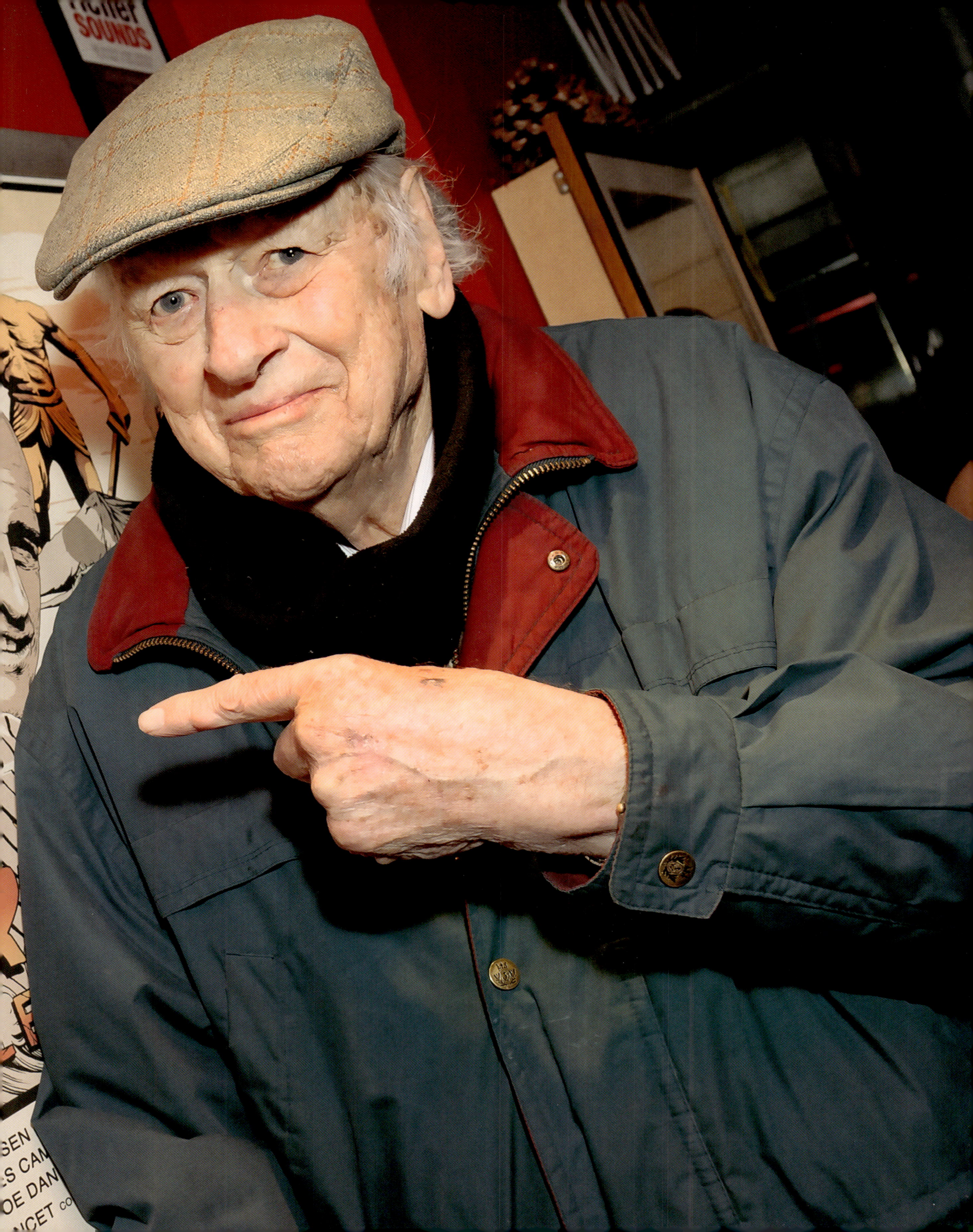
SOUNDS

THE RAY & DIANA HARRYHAUSEN FOUNDATION

When Ray Harryhausen died on 7th May 2013, aged 92, it was time to assess his work, his legacy and of course his vast collection that was spread over several locations and countries. In the years since his passing, the Foundation now has all the materials together for the very first time. Ray kept everything, a hoarder by today's standards. After more than sixty years of filmmaking, Ray's collection comprises of more than 50,000 items. Ranging from sketches, finished artwork, armatures, test footage, photos, negatives, books, bronze models, posters, studio memos, scripts, awards and all the creatures from his films. This is one of the most complete and comprehensive fantasy cinema and animation collections anywhere in the world, second only to the Walt Disney Company. Today there is a multimedia archive of film, tape and digital assets from commentary recordings I made with Ray about his films, as well as lost footage now found and scanned in 4k HD resolution.

Ray Harryhausen's creatures and films are legendary. The posters for his films are evocative and, as this books demonstrates, they are iconic images that have adorned both cinemas and bedroom walls for over half a century. Bringing them together for the first time in a single volume has been an enlightening experience. Many of the posters featured here are from our archive, but many are also from collectors — young and old — from around the world. This has been a collaborative effort and one which has motivated the fanbase. When Ray's films hit cinemas, from *Mighty Joe Young* in 1949 to *Clash of the Titans* in 1981, film posters had little or no monetary value. Most were simply

HARRYHAUSEN THE MOVIE POSTERS

discarded by cinemas or returned to distributors to be recycled. Thanks to the diligence, loyalty and admiration of the cinema-going public, this book is a definitive account of posters for Ray Harryhausen's films. Whilst we could not include every single variation, we have captured the very essence of these films through their imagery.

The stories behind the collecting of the posters are unique. For me it was sending a hand-written letter to the manager of my local Odeon Cinema in Woolwich, south London in 1981 that secured me a landscape quad of *Clash of the Titans,* which is framed in my office today.

For those fans who are familiar with the artwork from cinema and home video releases there is plenty more to see. The evolution of the posters and the campaigns makes this a fascinating read.

Proceeds from the sale of this book will go to the Ray and Diana Harryhausen Foundation to help with the delicate and ongoing restoration programme for the creature collection. Richard Holliss' hard work has unearthed fascinating and rare items years after they had been forgotten or discarded.

We achieved this full picture of Ray's film posters with the help and support of the fans and Richard Holliss' tireless research. Some posters were issued for a short run or as a double feature so would have a limited print run and be much rarer. I am delighted that Richard has written this book. His long association and friendship with Ray Harryhausen makes him the ideal author of this definitive work.

John Walsh, Trustee.
The Ray and Diana Harryhausen Foundation

THIS SPREAD: (Top Left) Three skeleton figures from *Jason and the Argonauts.* (Bottom Left) Ray, Foundation trustee John Walsh, and film director John Landis. (Right) Three of Ray's amazing stop-motion creatures: Mighty Joe Young (top), Medusa (middle) and Talos (bottom).

RICHARD'S ACKNOWLEDGMENTS

I'm indebted to the trustees and staff of the Ray and Diana Harryhausen Foundation (in particular, John Walsh, and Collection's Manager Connor Heaney), for their kindness and enthusiasm for the project, and for also making available items from Ray's personal archive. I'd also like to say a special thanks to collectors, Mike Hankin, Neil Pettigrew, Simon Greetham, Peter Douglass, Bruce Hershenson (emovieposter.com), and photographers, Andy Johnson and Mark Mawston for their invaluable assistance.

Other people who helped enormously with the book, either through the loan of material or overall support for the project, include Vanessa Harryhausen, Caroline Munro, John Landis, Allan Bryce, Mark Wolf, Alan Friswell, Alan Wightman, Archie Bryan, Colin Campbell, Enrico Altmann, Fabrizio Spurio, Ingo Strecker, Jan Willem, Jens Holzheuer, John V. Ulakovic, Julien Charra, Mike Siegel, Paul White, Richard Aeschlimann, Rod Bennett, Rolf Giesen, Scott McRae, Sheldon Hall, Wayne Kirk, Ted A. Bohus, Terry Eaton, Brian Sibley, Terry Michitsch, Nick Landau, Vivian Cheung, Angus Lamont, Asier Mensuro, Frazer Diamond, George Guzman, Greg Owens, Mark Pedersen, Mark Ulster, Michael Fett, René Meyer, Simon Harvey, Emma Wain, and last, but certainly not least, my editor Matt Ralphs, designer Natasha MacKenzie, and all the staff at Titan Books.

Remembering my parents, Patricia Marie, and Edward George Thomson, whose love of film was infectious, and two very dear friends, Ray and Diana Harryhausen.

CHPATER THIRTEEN **THE RAY & DIANA HARRYHAUSEN FOUNDATION**

SELECT INDEX

ABPC Elstree Studios	128, 129
Academy of Motion Picture Arts and Sciences	8
Allen, Irwin	46
Ameran Films	92
Animal World, The	44-49, 128
Arabian Nights	70, 104
Archer, Steven	168
Arrow Films	187
Associated British Cinemas (ABC)	29, 46, 61, 93, 129, 41
Ballester, Anselmo	11, 53, 61
Beast From 20,000 Fathoms, The	9, 26-33, 36, 46, 71, 187
Blue screen	71, 117, 161
Bradbury, Ray	29
British Board of Film Censors	29, 71
Burton, Tim	186
Bysouth, Brian	71
Cameron, James	8, 186, 187
Capitani, Alfredo	37, 93
Capra, Frank	14
Certificate A	129, 169
Certificate U	71
Certificate X	61
Chaffey, Don	105, 129
Chantrell, Tom	11, 129
Chester, Hal E.	29
Clash of the Titans	9, 10, 161, 166-181, 184, 187
Columbia Pictures	36, 53, 61, 70, 71, 93, 105, 117, 160, 161, 168
Computer Generated Graphics (CGI)	184
Cook, Randy	186
Cooper, Merian C.	15
Danforth, Jim	168
Dante, Joe	186
Davis, Desmond	168
Delgado, Marcel	15
del Toro, Guillermo	186
De Seta, Enrico	84
Dietz, Jack	28
Disman, Miloslav	161
Doré, Gustave	70
Dynamation	8, 71, 84, 93, 105, 117, 141, 152, 153
Dynarama	71, 152, 153, 161, 168, 186
Earth Vs. The Flying Saucers	52-59, 61
Elseviers, Raymond	141
Enfield, Cy	92
Eros	53
Evolution	46
First Men in the Moon	61, 104, 114-125, 152
Fischerova, O	11, 153
Flying Saucers from Outer Space	52
Foghorn, The	29
Force of the Trojans	184
Gadino, Victor	161
Gaumont Cinema Circuit	17, 71
Gilliam, Terry	186
Golden Voyage of Sinbad, The	71, 150-159, 160, 161
Goldhawk Studios	153
Gordon E. Sawyer Award	8
Gordon, Robert	36
Gorga, S.	169
Grauman's Chinese Theatre	8
Gulliver's Travels	84
Hammer Films	11, 29, 93, 128
Hanks, Tom	8
Harryhausen, Diana	186
Harryhausen, Vanessa	186
Hayward, Arthur	92, 105, 128, 141
Herrmann, Bernard	70, 84, 93, 105
Hessler, Gordon	153
Hildebrandt, Greg	11, 169
Hildebrandt, Tim	11, 169
Hollywood Boulevard	8
Hollywood Walk of Fame	8
Huyssen, Roger	169
It Came From Beneath the Sea	34-43, 61
Jackson, Peter	8, 186
Jason and the Argonauts	7, 8, 53, 84, 93, 102-112, 116, 117, 152, 153, 161, 168, 187
Juran, Nathan	61, 71, 117
Katzman, Sam	36
Keyhoe, Major Donald E.	52
Khuttula	71
King Kong	8, 14, 17, 29, 46
Kunstler, Mort	153
Landis, John	8, 186
Lassiter, John	186
Lee International Studios	161
Les Bowie Studios	93, 117, 129
Lettick, Birney	161
Lipniunas, V.	53
Lofgren, George	71
Lost World, The	14
Lourie, Eugene	29
Lucas, George	8, 186, 187
Martinati, Luigi	46
Mascii, Jean	93, 169
McCarthy, Frank	141
MGM Studios	71, 168, 169, 184
Mighty Joe Young	9, 12-25, 28, 29, 161, 187
Morningside Productions	61, 128
Mother Goose Stories, The	14, 186
Munro, Caroline	186
Muren, Dennis	186
Mysterious Island	11, 84, 92-101, 104, 116, 117
Mysterious Island, The (novel)	92, 116
Napoli, Bruno	169
National Screen Services	93
Neugebauer, J	153
O'Brien, Willis	14, 46, 140
O'Connolly, James	140
Odeon Cinemas	71, 84, 105, 117, 153, 161, 169
One Million B.C. (1940)	128
One Million Years B.C. (1966)	11, 53, 71, 105, 126-139, 141, 161, 187
Pal, George	14
Panavision	71, 117
Park, Nick	186
Penso, Gilles	186, 187
Picchioni, Franco	141
Pinewood Studios	168
Poncet, Alexandre	186, 187
Puppetoons	14
Rank Film Organisation	84, 161
Rau, Charles	105
Ray and Diana Harryhausen Foundation, The	187, 190-191
Ray Harryhausen: Special Effects Titan	182-189
Rehberger, Gustav	46
RKO	9, 15
Schneer, Charles H.	36, 46, 52, 71, 92, 105, 116, 117, 128, 129, 140, 153, 160, 168
Schoedsack, Ernest B.	15
Sears, Fred	53
Seven Arts Productions	128, 140, 141
7th Voyage of Sinbad, The	68-81, 84, 92, 104, 105, 152, 153, 161, 187
Sevilla Film Studios	84
Shepperton Studios	105, 117, 141
Sher, Jack	84
Sinbad and the Eye of the Tiger	11, 160-165, 168
Sodium Vapor System	84, 105
Soubie, Roger	117
Spielberg, Steven	8, 186
Stop-motion animation	8, 14, 15, 28, 29, 37, 53, 71, 93, 104, 117, 128, 141, 153, 184
Super Dynamation	71
Swift, Jonathan	84
Technicolor	71
3 Worlds of Gulliver, The	71, 84-91
Thurston, Jack	129
20 Million Miles to Earth	60-67, 70, 161, 187
Valley of Gwangi, The	15, 140-149, 152, 187
Valley of the Mist	28
Verne, Jules	92
Verona Studios	153
Vonderwerth	71
Wanamaker, Sam	160
War of the Worlds, The (novel)	28, 52
Warner Brothers	29, 46, 140, 141
Walsh, John	190-191
Wells, H. G.	28, 52, 116, 117
Why We Fight	14
Wilson, Joe	187

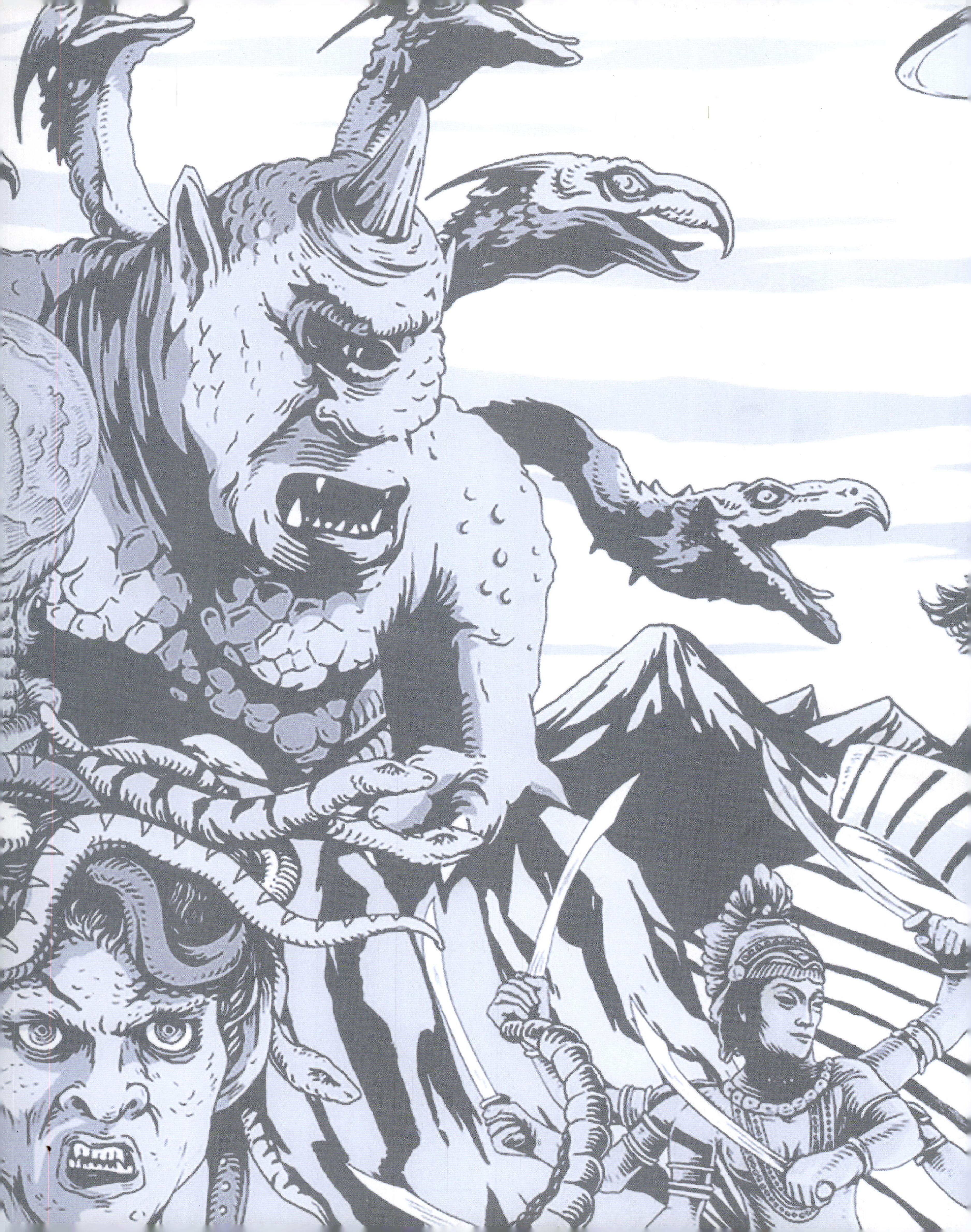